Collins

Science Expert 2

Authors
Meenakshi Atal
Debahuti Das

Preface

Collins Science Expert is a series of 14 coursebooks for Classes 1 to 8. The coursebooks for grades 1 and 2 are aligned with Environmental Studies (EVS) and grades 3 to 5 with Science. For Classes 6 to 8, there are separate coursebooks for Physics, Chemistry and Biology. This series, which is the revised edition of *Science Panorama*, is based on the **latest curriculum** prescribed by the **Council for the Indian School Certificate Examinations** and adheres to the guidelines of the National Education Policy (NEP) 2020.

In line with the curriculum, a thematic, coherent and structured approach has been followed and all new topics suggested in the curriculum have been included. The series also caters to the three domains of learning—**cognitive** (*intellectual nature*), **affective** (*attitudinal nature*) and **psychomotor** (*actionable nature*).

Aimed to answer a learner's cry: '*Teach me the way I want to learn*', this series adopts a method—**visual**, **auditory**, **kinesthetic** and **tactile** (**VAKT**)—that caters to all kinds of learners. Keeping in mind the saying 'I hear – I forget, I see – I understand and I do – I remember', a lot of hands-on activities have been incorporated. This would enable learners to understand and learn scientific concepts through experiential learning.

This series also emphasizes on developing *scientific skills* such as **observation**, **data collection**, **investigation**, **estimation**, **prediction**, **analysis** and **drawing inferences**. This would help in developing a scientific temperament in learners from a young age. The series also draws a connection between cause and effect; and focuses on the application of concepts in real-life situations. The language used is child-friendly and age-appropriate. Sufficient examples from everyday life have been given to help learners understand the concepts. A lot of colourful illustrations and well-labelled diagrams have been included to engage learners and aid in their understanding.

We would like to take this opportunity to thank all the teachers who reviewed the books and provided their valuable feedback, which helped in improving the quality of the content.

Any suggestions or constructive criticism from the users are welcome. We shall try to incorporate those in the future editions.

Authors

Key Features

The key features of ***Collins Science Expert*** series are completely aligned with *National Education Policy* (NEP) 2020. These meticulously designed key features, based on VAKT (visual, auditory, kinesthetic and tactile) learning style and the three domains of Bloom's Taxonomy which include **cognitive (intellectual skills)**, **affective (attitudinal nature)** and **psychomotor (actionable nature)**, can be used as learning strategies to help in the development of scientific and 21st Century Skills in students. These key features also aim to help students shift from rote-learning to competency-based learning.

Bloom's Taxonomy

Cognitive Domain

- Focuses on intellectual skills such as critical thinking, problem solving, and creating a knowledge base
- Expects learners to progress linearly, beginning at "remember" and ending at "create."

Features:

- Prior Knowledge
- Learning Objectives
- Let's Get Started
- Quick Revision
- Talk Time
- Concept Map
- Keywords
- Exercise
- Word to know
- Review Corner

Affective Domain

- Focuses on the attitudes, values, interests and appreciation of learners
- Focuses on allowing learners to understand what their own values are and how they have developed

Features:

- Greenathon
- Skill Booster
- Worksheets
- My Environment, My Responsibility!
- Happy Accidents
- Innovation: The Steppingstone
- Role of Science in Benefitting the Society

Psycho motor Domain

- Encompasses the ability of learners to physically accomplish tasks and perform movement and skills
- Expects learners to progress from using reflexes and basic movement to non-discursive communication and meaningfully expressive activity

Features:

- Do It Yourself
- Activities
- Skill Booster
- Worksheets
- My Eco Craft
- Innovation: The Steppingstone
- STEAM Worksheets

Skills and Learnings

Colour-coded tags and icons are used to easily identify the types of skills and learnings being addressed.

NEP Aligned Skills

21st Century Skills (21CS)

Learning Skills

- Critical Thinking
- Creativity and Innovation
- Collaboration
- Communication

Life Skills

- Flexibility and Adaptability
- Leadership and Responsibility
- Initiative and Self-direction
- Productivity and Accountability
- Social and Cross-cultural Interaction

Literacy Skills

- Information Literacy
- Media Literacy
- Technology Literacy

SUSTAINABLE DEVELOPMENT GOALS

Experiential Learning (EL)

Cross Curricular (CC)

Bloom's Taxonomy (BT)

Art Integration (AI)

India Focus (IF)

SEE Learning

About the Features

Be a Scientist! (Classes 3 to 5): Introduction to science process skills to help develop scientific attitudes

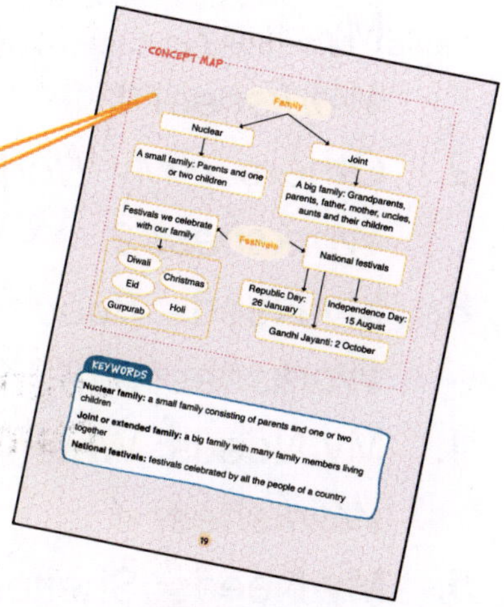

- **Concept Map:** Snapshot of the chapter in the form of a graphic organizer for quick recapitulation
- **Keywords:** Definitions of important terms

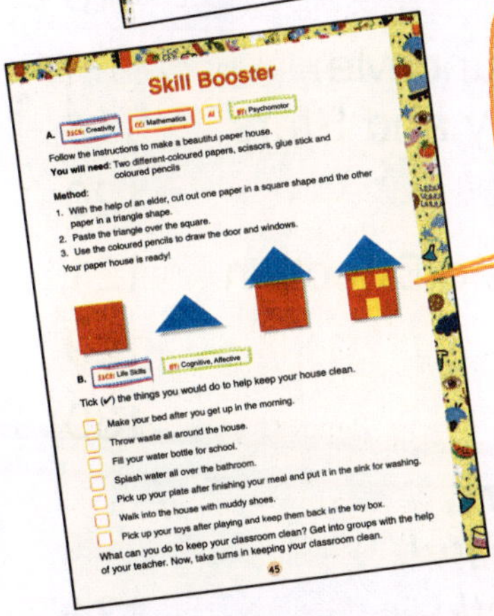

Skill Booster: Section aimed at imparting 21st Century Skills alongwith a focus on Cross-curricular Links, India Focus, Art Integration, Experiential Learning and Bloom's Taxonomy

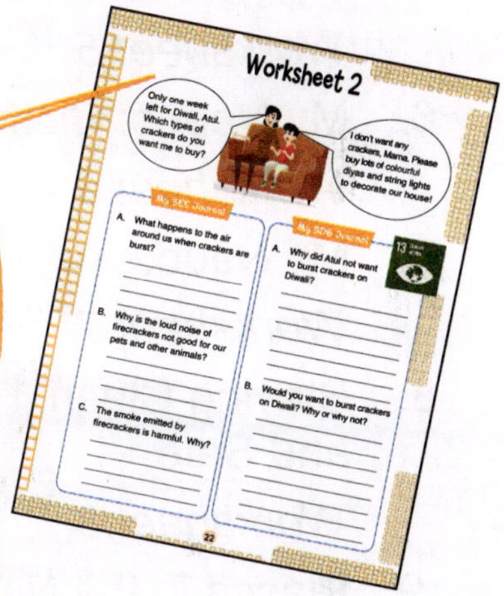

Worksheet: Interesting questions imparting skills catering to social, emotional and ethical (SEE) needs and United Nations' sustainable development goals (SDGs)

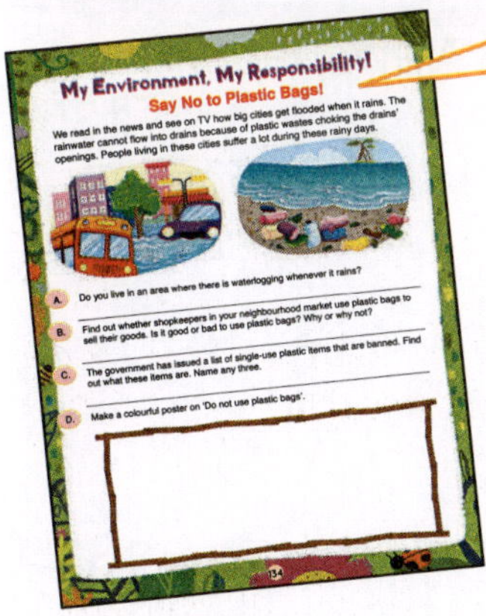

My Environment, My Responsibility! (Classes 1 and 2): Special pages to spread awareness and a sense of responsibility towards the environment

Happy Accidents (Classes 3 to 8): Interesting snippets on discoveries and inventions by chance/accidents that led to beneficial ways

STEAM Worksheets (Classes 6 to 8): Interesting project ideas integrating Science, Technology, Engineering, Arts and Mathematics to solve real-world problems

My Eco Craft (Classes 1 and 2): Hands-on activities to enhance learning beyond the classroom

Innovation: The Steppingstone (Classes 3 to 5): Ideas to guide students to solve real-life problems in innovative ways

Role of Science in Benefitting the Society (Classes 6 to 8): Snippets on the contributions made by various scientists for the development of the society

Find Out: Research-oriented questions requiring learners to look beyond the classroom

What do we call the person who treats our pet dog when it falls sick?

FIND OUT

Contents

1 My Body

Prior Knowledge

- Names of different parts of our body
- Names and functions of sense organs

Learning Objectives

- Sense organs and the work they do
- Organs and their functions
- How to take care of the body

LET'S GET STARTED

Match the body parts in the picture to their names.

Nose | Head

Eye | Ear

Neck | Mouth

Hand | Leg

A POEM!

Sing with actions.

The Hokey Pokey

You put your
right hand in,
You put your
right hand out,
You put your
right hand in,
And shake it all about,
You do the hokey pokey
and turn yourself around
That's what it's all about.

Repeat the lines with your left hand, right foot and left foot.

Our body has many parts. These parts are also called organs. All these organs work together to help our body function.

SENSE ORGANS AND THE WORK THEY DO

In Class 1, we have learnt about our sense organs.

There are five sense organs—ears, eyes, nose, skin and tongue. Ears help us hear, eyes help us see, the nose helps us smell, the skin helps us feel and the tongue helps us taste the food we eat.

DO YOU KNOW?

The skin is the largest organ of our body!

Eyes

Nose

Tongue

Skin

Ears

DO IT YOURSELF

Feely Bag Activity

Find a few things to put in your feely bag. Ask your friend to close his/her eyes and guess what is inside. Your friend can smell, feel or even try to hear the sound by gently hitting or tossing it around (No tasting, please!).

- We should wash our eyes with cold water every morning.
- We should not read in dim light.
- We should keep our ears clean.
- We should clean our tongue with a tongue cleaner every time we brush our teeth.

QUICK REVISION

Name the following.

1. A man rang the bell to deliver pizza. Which sense organ helped you know this? ____________
2. The smell of pizza filled the room. Which sense organ helped you know this? ____________
3. The pizza looked delicious! It had capsicum, tomato and cheese. Which sense organ helped you know this? ____________
4. As you took a slice of the pizza, you could feel it was hot. Which sense organ helped you know this? ____________
5. The pizza was spicy. Which sense organ helped you know this? ____________

OTHER BODY PARTS

Press your left arm with your right hand. You will feel some parts are soft and some parts are hard. Now, slowly feel the different parts of your body to feel the hard and the soft parts. The hard parts are your bones, while the soft parts are your muscles.

Bones

The bones give shape and support to our body. The **bones** in our body together form a structure called **skeleton**. The skeleton protects the organs inside our body.

A newborn baby has 300 bones. Some of these bones join as the baby grows. An adult has 206 bones.

Joints

A **joint** is a place where two bones meet.

Touch your elbow and feel the joint. We can move different parts of our body because of the joints. Joints help us move, bend or twist. You can bend your fingers to write because of the joints.

Muscles

The soft part of the body that lie under the skin are called **muscles**. Muscles are attached to the bones and together they help us move. There are more than 600 muscles in our body. Muscles help us walk, sit, jump, run and do other actions. They also help us maintain a good posture.

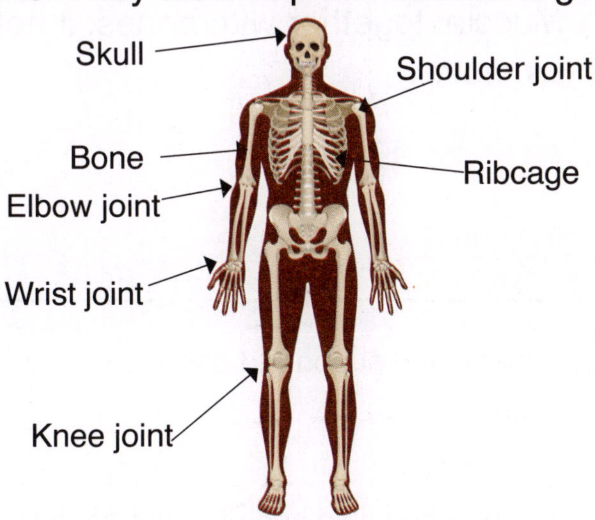

Skeleton

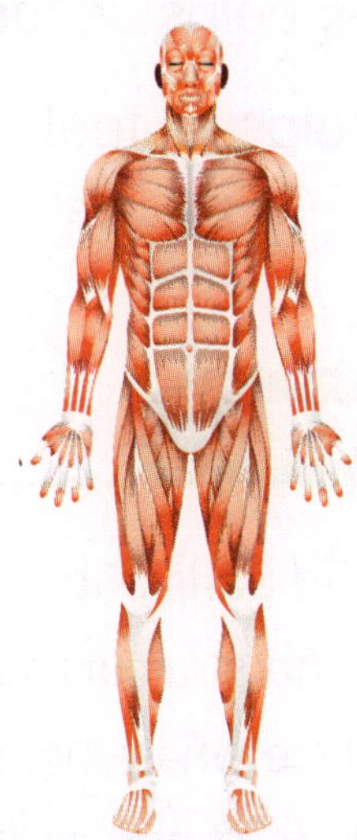

Muscles

TAKING CARE OF THE BODY

We should take good care of our body. We should keep our bones and muscles healthy. Here are some of the ways to take care of our body.

Eat healthy food.

Drink lots of water.

Exercise regularly.

Take enough rest.

CONCEPT MAP

Our Body

- **Sense Organs**
  - Nose: helps us smell
  - Ears: helps us hear
  - Eyes: helps us see
  - Tongue: helps us taste
  - Skin: helps us feel
- **Some Parts of Our Body**
  - Bone: hard part of our body
  - Skeleton: found inside our body
  - Joint: a place where two bones meet
  - Muscle: together with bones, it helps us move

KEYWORDS

Bones: hard parts of our body that give shape and support to our body

Skeleton: the structure formed by our bones

Joint: a place where bones meet

Muscle: the soft part of the body that lies under the skin and over the bones

Exercise

Objective Type Questions

A. Fill in the blanks.

1. We taste food with our ______________ (tongue/nose).
2. The organ that helps us see is the ______________ (eye/brain).
3. ______________ (Hands/Bones) give shape and support to our body.
4. A joint is a place where two ______________ (bones/muscles) meet.

B. Write T for True and F for False.

1. Eyes help us walk. ◯
2. The skeleton protects the organs inside our body. ◯
3. Muscles help us move, bend or twist. ◯
4. To take care of our body, we need to exercise and rest. ◯

Subjective Type Questions

Answer the following questions.

1. What are bones and skeleton?

____

2. What is a joint?

____

3. How does a skeleton help us?

____

4. What are muscles? How do they help us?

____

____

5. Write two ways in which you can take care of your body.

____

____

Application-based Question

Have you seen police officers with dogs at the airports or at railway stations? How do these dogs help police officers?

Picture-based Question

Draw a line to match each sense organ to its correct picture. One has been done for you.

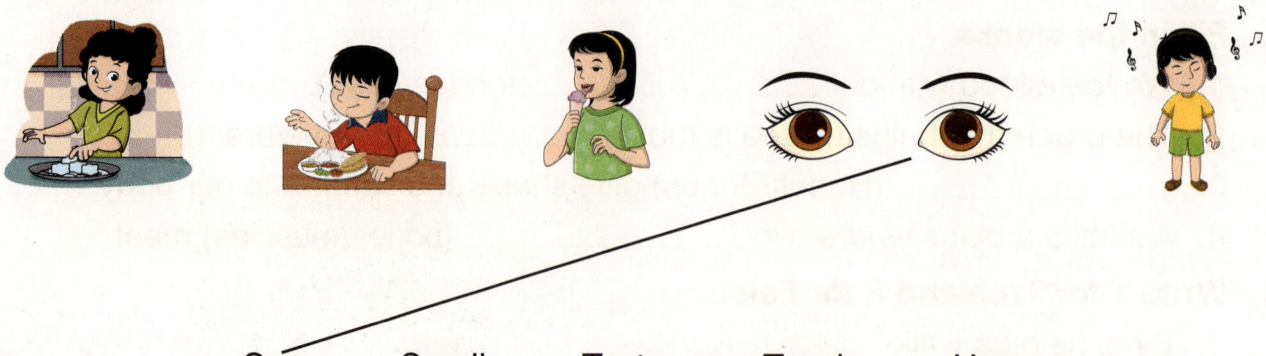

See Smell Taste Touch Hear

Skill Booster

21CS: Critical Thinking | **BT:** Cognitive, Affective

Once, many body organs were fighting. Each one felt it was more important than the others.

The eyes said, 'Without me, you cannot see the world.'

The bones said, 'Without me, you cannot stand.'

The muscles said, 'Without me, you cannot move.'

The joint said, 'Without me, you will not be able to move your arms and legs.'

And the nose said, 'Without me, you will not be able to breathe.'

Who do you think is the most important? Tick (✔) the correct option.

a. Eyes b. Nose c. Joint

d. Bones e. Muscles f. All are equally important

Worksheet 1

The students of Class 2 went on a picnic to a nature park. It was a large, beautiful park with many trees and flowering plants. There was a large rose garden with many kinds of roses. Various birds, bees and butterflies were flying around them. After playing, they had snacks under a large tree.

My SEE Journal

A. What things did the students see in the park?

B. What colours of roses did they see in the garden?

My SDG Journal

15 LIFE ON LAND

A. What should the children do with the empty food packets and plastic water bottles?

B. How can you take care of the park you play in?

2 Others in My World

Prior Knowledge

- My family
- Celebration of special days with our family

Learning Objectives

- Nuclear family and extended family
- Fun with family and friends
- Celebration of events and festivals
- Caring and sharing
- Care for pets

LET'S GET STARTED

Paste or draw pictures of your family members to complete the family tree given below.

Your Family Tree

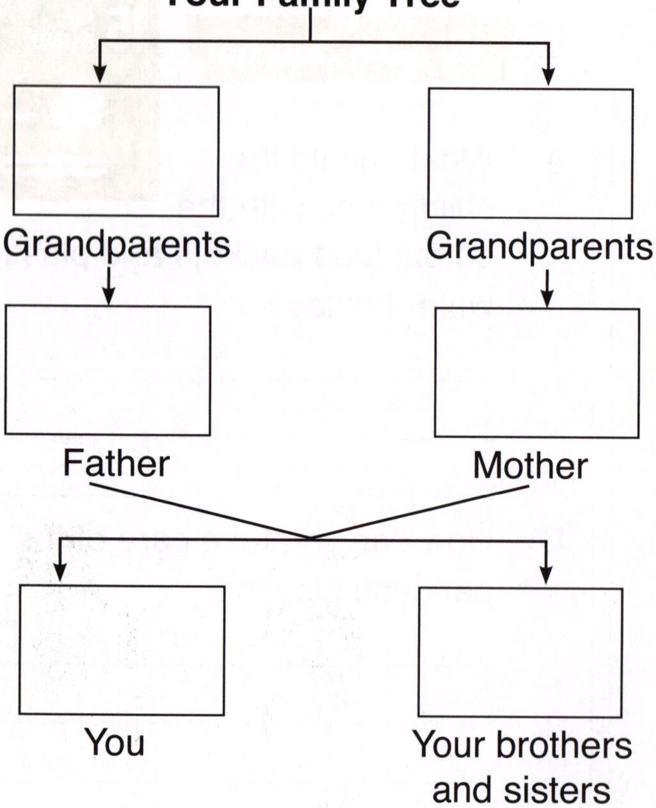

In Class 1, you have learnt about small and big families. A small family is one where only the parents live together with their one or two children. Such a family is called a **nuclear** family.

A big family where grandparents, father, mother, uncles, aunts as well as their children live together is called a **joint** or **extended** family. The members of a joint family eat together, have fun together, and they also help and respect each other.

FESTIVALS WE CELEBRATE

Members of a family celebrate special events and festivals together. Some of the festivals we celebrate are given below.

Diwali

Diwali is the festival of lights. We clean our homes and decorate them with small lights and diyas. We also make colourful rangolis. We wear new clothes and exchange gifts and sweets.

GREENATHON

We must celebrate a 'Green Diwali' by not bursting crackers. The smoke produced by bursting crackers is harmful for the health of all living beings. The loud noise of bursting crackers scares away birds and other animals.

Christmas

Christmas is celebrated on 25 December. It is considered to be the birthday of Jesus Christ. We decorate a Christmas tree in our homes. Families and friends get together, go to church and have a meal together. We exchange gifts, too.

Eid

On Eid, we wear new clothes and hug each other and wish '*Eid Mubarak*'. We go to a mosque to pray. A special sweet dish, called *sewaiyan,* is made on this day. Families and their friends get together to celebrate.

Gurpurab

Gurpurabs are festivals for the gurus. Guru nanak's birthday is celebrated as one of the Gurpurabs. On this day, we go to a Gurdwara. We pray together and eat together too. A big free kitchen, called 'langar', is set up to serve food to all who come. Families help in serving the food. A special *halwa* is served to all.

There are many other festivals such as Cheiraoba, Bihu, Durga Puja, Ganesh Chaturthi, Buddha Purnima, Mahavir Jayanti, Pongal, Vishu, Baisakhi, Easter, Guddi Padwa and Navroze that are celebrated in our country. Find out more about these from your friends/neighbours who celebrate them.

FIND OUT

Holi

Holi is also called the festival of colours. We celebrate it with our families, friends and neighbours. We apply colours to each other's face and body. A special sweet dish called *gujiya* is made on this day.

NATIONAL FESTIVALS

National festivals are the festivals celebrated by all the people of a country. In India, we celebrate three main national festivals. These are Republic Day, Independence Day and Gandhi Jayanti.

Festival	When do We Celebrate it?	Why is it Celebrated?
Republic Day	26 January	It is the day the Rule Book of India (Constitution of India) was given to the people.
Independence Day	15 August	It is the day India became a free country.
Gandhi Jayanti	2 October	It is the birthday of Mahatma Gandhi, the father of our Nation.

QUICK REVISION

Write T for True and F for False.

1. People make colourful rangolis on Christmas. ◯
2. Christmas is the birthday of Jesus Christ. ◯
3. During Holi, a special dish called *sewaiyan* is made. ◯
4. Republic Day is our national festival. ◯

CELEBRATING DIFFERENCES

We see many people around us. Do they look the same? Do all of them have the same hobbies?

Look at the pictures given alongside.

Talk about how these children are similar to you. How are they different from you and why? Now, write them down in the boxes given here.

TALK TIME

Talk about what you are good at and not so good at.

Similiar	Different
____________	____________
____________	____________
____________	____________
____________	____________

We all look different. Our likes and dislikes as well as our hobbies are different.

We must respect each other. We should help people around us, especially those who are not able to do things in the same way that we do.

> **TALK TIME**
> Do your grandparents live with you? If yes, how do you spend time with them?

We should always respect and help old people. At home, our grandparents too may need our help and care. We should spend time with them. They tell stories, read to us, play with us and teach us how and why to put things at their proper places.

Playing Games Together

We love to play games with our friends and family. Games keep us happy and busy.

Make a list of all the indoor and outdoor games you like to play.

When we are playing with friends and family, we should select a game that can be played by everyone so that no one feels left out.

Indoor Games

Outdoor Games

PET CARE

Our pet is a part of our family. Some people keep a dog to play with as well as to guard their houses. Some people keep cats for company. Other pets can include birds, rabbits, turtles and fish.

To keep our pet healthy and happy, we have to look after it, just as we look after ourselves. We must bathe it, feed it and take it for regular health checkups.

A boy with his pet

A caring family is a happy family!

CONCEPT MAP

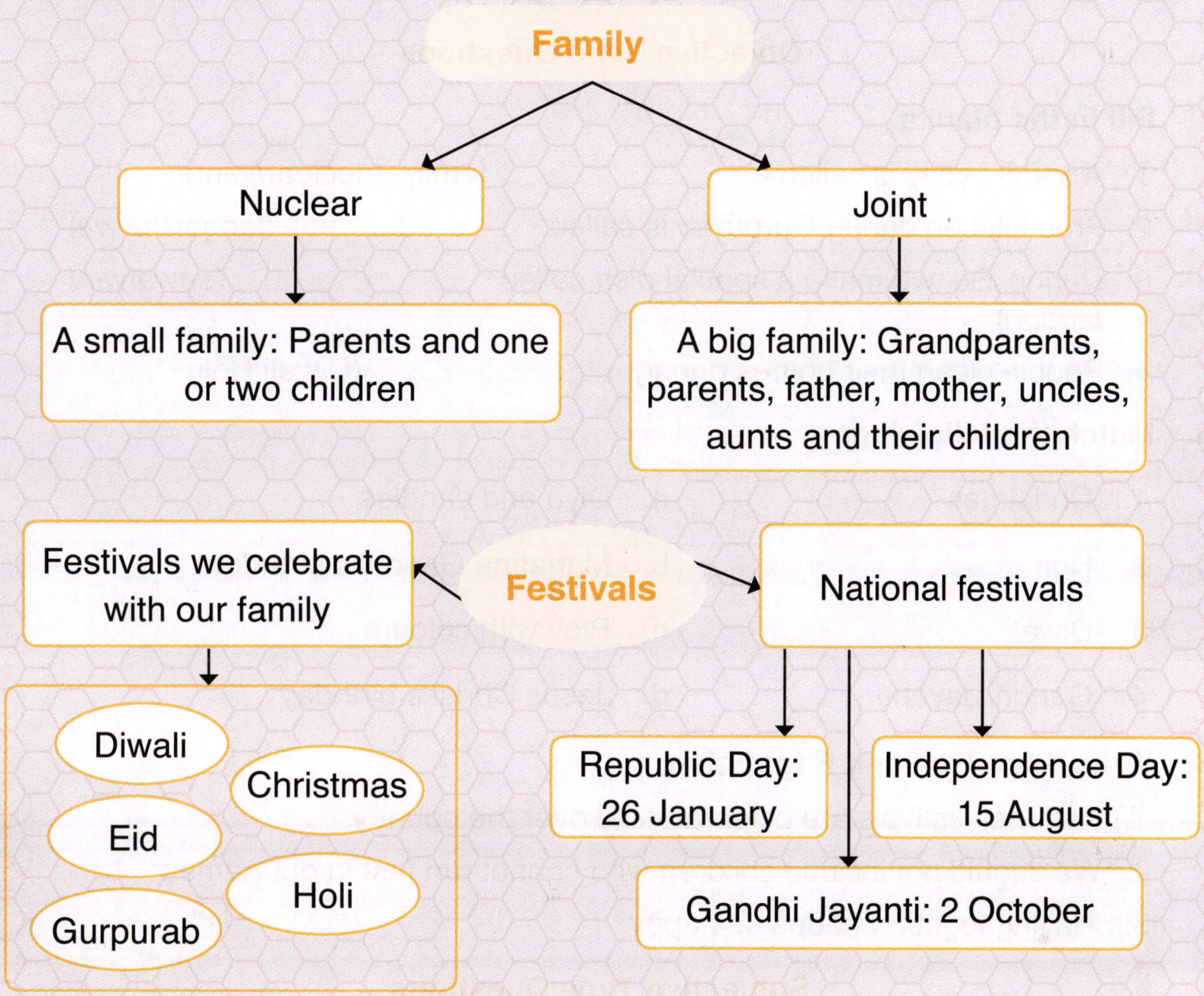

KEYWORDS

Nuclear family: a small family consisting of parents and one or two children

Joint or extended family: a big family with many family members living together

National festivals: festivals celebrated by all the people of a country

Exercise

Objective Type Questions

A. Fill in the blanks.

1. A small family is called a ______________ family. (nuclear/joint)
2. Free kitchen during Gurpurab is called ______________. (langar/*halwa*)
3. During Eid, we make a special dish called ______________. (*sewaiyan*/ *laddoo*)
4. People clean their homes during ______________. (Diwali/Holi)

B. Match the following.

1. Christmas	a. Diya and candles
2. Holi	b. Mahatma Gandhi's birthday
3. Diwali	c. Play with colours
4. Gandhi Jayanti	d. Jesus Christ's birthday

C. Write T for True and F for False.

1. National festivals are celebrated all over the country. ◯
2. We should not include children who cannot run fast in our games. ◯
3. Playing together keeps us happy. ◯

Subjective Type Questions

Answer the following questions.

1. What is a joint family?

____

2. Name any two national festivals. When are they celebrated?

____

3. Which is your favourite festival? How do you celebrate it?

____

4. How can we look after our pet?

____

Application-based Question

How are national festivals different from other festivals?

Picture-based Question

Name the festivals given below.

____________ ____________ ____________ ____________ ____________

Skill Booster

A. 21CS: Creativity | CC: Mathematics | BT: Psychomotor

Make a Paper Rangoli!

Fold a square paper two times. Now, cut out a small design using your scissors with the help of an elder. Make sure the folds are joined while cutting out a design. Open the page to find your rangoli design.

B. 21CS: Life Skills | CC: English | AI | BT: Affective, Psychomotor

Make a Card!

We wish each other during festivals. We send cards to people who stay far away. So, here is an idea to make a card. Take a white sheet (or chart paper). Fold it in half, exactly. Ask an elder to cut an okra or lady's fingers. Dip the cut end in differently-coloured paints and press it on the card. Make a design of your own.
Write a nice message inside.

C. 21CS: Critical Thinking | BT: Cognitive, Affective

During festivals, we all have fun, and sometimes, we burst crackers. However Ringo, the pet, does not enjoy it. Why do you think so?

Worksheet 2

My SEE Journal

A. What happens to the air around us when crackers are burst?

____

____

____

____

B. Why is the loud noise of firecrackers not good for our pets and other animals?

____

____

____

____

C. The smoke emitted by firecrackers is harmful. Why?

____

____

____

____

My SDG Journal

13 CLIMATE ACTION

A. Why did Atul not want to burst crackers on Diwali?

____

____

____

____

____

____

____

B. Would you want to burst crackers on Diwali? Why or why not?

____

____

____

____

____

____

____

____

3 My Needs: Food

Prior Knowledge

- Food from plants
- Food from animals
- Good food and staying healthy

Learning Objectives

- Need for food
- Go, grow and glow food
- Water
- Balanced diet
- Junk food
- Healthy eating habits
- Different kinds of food and diets

LET'S GET STARTED

Chhavi is confused about what she should eat for breakfast.

Help her pick out the food items that you think she should eat for breakfast.

Food items for Chhavi

1. ____________________
2. ____________________
3. ____________________
4. ____________________

NEED FOR FOOD

All living things need food to live. Food gives us energy to work and play. Food makes us healthy, fit and strong. We get food from plants and animals.

Fruits

Vegetables

Food from plants

Milk, meat, eggs and fish

Food from animals

GO, GROW AND GLOW FOOD

We need to eat different kinds of food to stay healthy and fit. The food that we eat can be arranged into different groups. The different food groups are given below.

Go Food

This kind of food gives us the energy to work and play. It is also called **energy-giving food**. Rice, bread, cheese, honey, potato and butter are some examples.

DO YOU KNOW?

'Go food' is also called **carbohydrates**. 'Grow food' is also known as **proteins**. 'Glow food' is also known as **vitamins**.

Bread

Potatoes

Butter

Honey

Cheese

Our breakfast should contain a lot of 'Go food' so that we get energy for the entire day to do various activities. A sportsperson's diet should also be rich in 'Go food' because they need a lot of energy.

Grow Food

This kind of food is needed for our body to grow. It is also called **body-building food**. Milk, meat, fish, eggs and pulses are some examples.

Milk

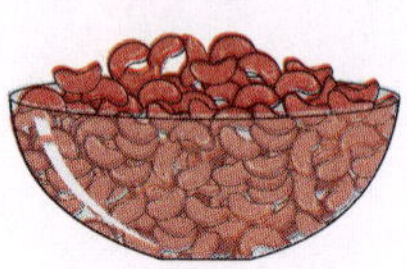

Pulses

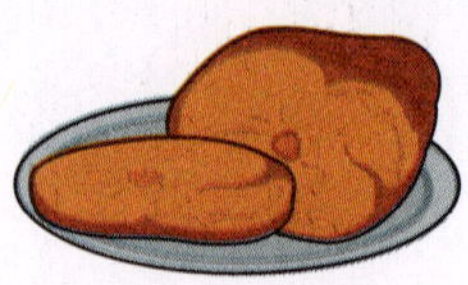

Meat

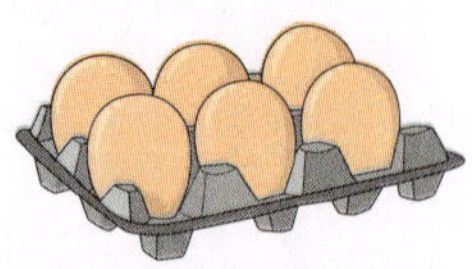

Eggs

Glow Food

This kind of food protects us from falling sick. It is also called **protective food**. It keeps our teeth, bones, eyes, skin and hair healthy. Fruits and green leafy vegetables are some examples.

Fruits and vegetables

QUICK REVISION

Tick (✔) the food items that you can eat raw and cross (✘) the ones that need to be cooked.

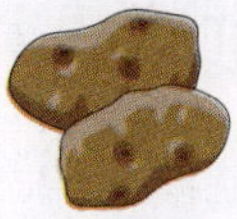 ◯

Potatoes

 ◯

Orange

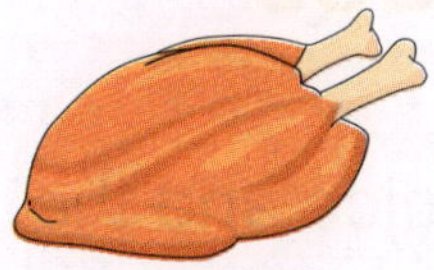 ◯

Meat

 ◯

Cucumber

WATER

We cannot live without water. Water helps us digest the food we eat. It also helps flush out waste from our body.

DO YOU KNOW?

We must drink 8 to 10 glasses of water every day.

Food Etiquette!

Never play with your fork, spoon and other cutlery items.

Start eating only after everybody is served.

Always chew with your mouth closed.

BALANCED DIET

We should eat food from all the food groups.

A diet that has the right amount of food from every food group is called a **balanced diet**. It helps us stay fit and healthy.

JUNK FOOD

Some food items are tasty but add very little value to our health. Such food items are called **junk food**.

We should avoid eating junk food.

Avoid eating junk food

HEALTHY EATING HABITS

- Wash your hands before and after meals.
- Eat food at regular intervals.
- Always eat freshly cooked food. Eat fresh fruits and vegetables.
- Chew your food well.
- Never waste food. Take only as much as you can eat.
- Do not overeat.

TALK TIME

Your mummy, daddy, grandmother or any other family member might be making a particular dish better than anybody you know.

Tell your friends about this dish! Mention the name of the dish, what it is made of, how often you eat it, why you like it.

DIFFERENT KINDS OF FOOD AND DIETS

What we like to eat is our choice and the choice of the family.

Food that comes from plants are part of a **vegetarian** diet. Food that comes from animals, specially meat and fish, are part of a **non-vegetarian** diet.

In some places, people have rice more often than chapattis. In some other places, people eat chapattis more often than rice. This is because people mostly eat what grows in and around the places they live.

Different kinds of food

The choice of food also differs for people of different ages. Children love to eat different kinds of food. Grown-ups are more careful about the kind of food they eat. Old people follow specific diets that are based on their health. Their diet may contain non-spicy and non-oily food.

We must respect other people's food choices.

CONCEPT MAP

Kinds of Food

Go Food: energy giving food such as rice, bread, cheese

Grow Food: body build-ing food such as milk, meat, fish

Junk food: tasty food but not good for health

Glow Food: protective food such as fruits and green leafy vegetables

KEYWORDS

Balanced diet: the right amount of food from all groups

Vegetarian diet: food that comes from plants

Omnivorous diet: food that comes from animals, specially meat and fish

Exercise

Objective Type Questions

A. Fill in the blanks.

1. Food gives us ________________ (money/energy).
2. The three food groups are ________________ (Slow/Go) food, ________________ (Grow/Throw) food and ________________ (Flow/Glow) food.
3. Breakfast should have a lot of ________________ (Grow/Go) food.
4. Water helps us ________________ (digest/chew) food.

B. Write T for True and F for False.

1. A sportsperson needs to eat a lot of Glow food. ◯
2. Grow food protects us from falling sick. ◯
3. We should eat a balanced diet. ◯
4. Eating junk food regularly makes us healthy. ◯
5. We should make noise while chewing our food. ◯

Subjective Type Questions

Answer the following questions.

1. Write two healthy eating habits.

____

____

2. How does water help us?

____

____

Application-based Questions

A. Seema only likes to eat cakes and ice creams. Why does her mother tell her eating only cakes and ice creams is not good for her?

B. Why should we always keep our food covered when we are not eating?

Picture-based Question

Match the pictures to the food groups. One has been done for you.

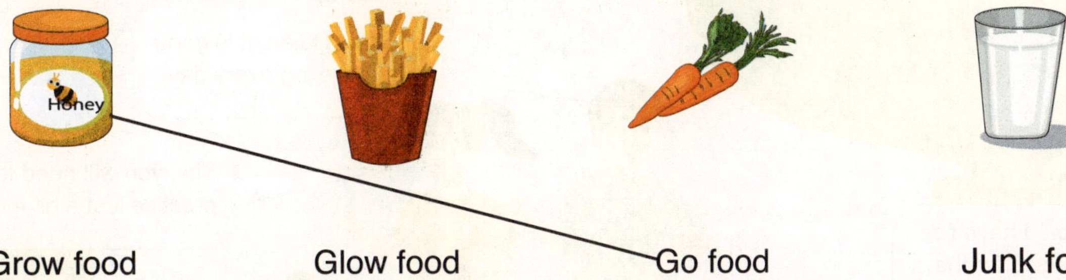

Grow food Glow food Go food Junk food

Skill Booster

A. 21CS: Creativity and Innovation | BT: Psychomotor

Decorate the dining table by making a banana octopus and surprise your guests! Peel a banana carefully. Slice off half the banana. Now, with an elder's help, carefully slit the peel into eight sections. Push two cloves between the banana skin to make them look like eyes. Place the banana on a plate to make your banana octopus.

B. 21CS: Critical Thinking | AI | BT: Cognitive, Psychomotor

Do you know that food comes in different colours? Redraw the pictures given below on a chart paper. Colour the pictures given below to match their colours with some of the colours from the rainbow!

Apple

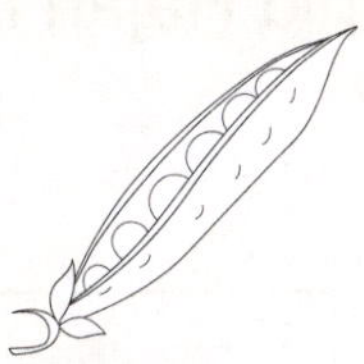
Peas

Brinjal

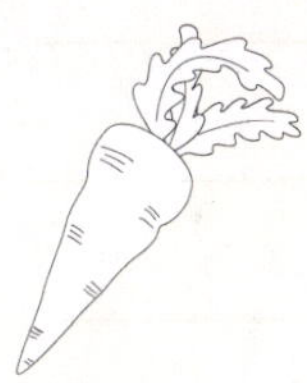
Carrot

Corn

Blueberry

C. 21CS: Collaboration, Life Skills | CC: Health and Physical Education | BT: Cognitive, Affective

Make a healthy fruit salad!

Ask an elder to chop different fruits for you. Put them in a big bowl and add some vanilla ice cream to it. Mix well. Your tasty fruit salad is ready. You can bring your salad to school and share it with your friends. Some people do not get enough food for even one meal. So, if you are about to waste food, think of these people and stop. Take only that much food in your plate that you can eat.

Worksheet 3

My SEE Journal

A. For Rajan to have the energy to exercise properly, what type of food should his parents cook for him?

____

____

____

____

B. To prevent tiredness, what should Rajan do apart from having healthy food?

____

____

____

____

My SDG Journal

3 GOOD HEALTH AND WELL-BEING

A. Rajan wanted to remain fit and healthy for Sports Day. When his elder sister wanted to have burgers and pizza, Rajan refused. He told his mother he wanted a home-cooked meal. Why did Rajan refuse such a tasty meal?

____

____

____

B. Should you take care of your body only before competitions?

____

____

4 My Needs: Water

Prior Knowledge

- Uses of water in the family
- Sources of water at home
- Sources of water in the surroundings
- Need for storage of water

Learning Objectives

- Uses of water
- Sources of water
- Importance of clean water
- How to keep water clean
- Saving and reusing water

LET'S GET STARTED

Look at the pictures given below and fill in the missing letters to complete their names.

1. Water falls down from clouds as R _ I _

2. Water flows down the mountains as R _ V _ R

USES OF WATER

Water is needed by all living things. Human beings, plants and animals need water to live, grow and keep their bodies healthy and clean.

> **FIND OUT** Can you think of some more uses of water? Mention any two.

Here are some daily activities for which we need water.

Drinking

Bathing

Washing

Cooking

SOURCES OF WATER

Rain is the main source of water on Earth. It is also the purest form of water.

Rain filling up a stream

Rainwater fills lakes, ponds, rivers, streams, seas and oceans. These waterbodies are also sources of water.

Some rainwater seeps into the soil. This is called groundwater. People dig wells and use a hand pump to draw out groundwater.

Well

Hand pump

Tap

CLEAN WATER

In our homes, we get water when we turn on the taps. This water is brought by pipes from the water supply station to our homes. At the water supply station, it is cleaned and made safe for our use.

It is important to clean drinking water to kill germs. We might fall ill if we consume it. We should boil water or use a water filter to purify drinking water.

Boiling water

A water filter

All the food we eat has water. During summer, we should eat more fruits and vegetables that have a lot of water such as watermelon, cucumber, pineapple, oranges and grapes. This will fulfill our body's need for water to some extent.

Cucumber

Watermelon

Pineapple

Orange

Grapes

KEEPING WATER CLEAN

Some ways in which we can keep water clean are given below.

- We should never throw garbage in ponds, rivers, lakes, etc.
- Factories should not let their waste flow into rivers and lakes.
- We should not bathe or wash our clothes in ponds, lakes and rivers.

QUICK REVISION

Name the following.

1. The main source of water ______________
2. Water that seeps into the ground ______________
3. A fruit that contains water ______________

SAVE AND REUSE WATER

- Do not leave water taps running.
- Use a mug of water to rinse your mouth while brushing your teeth.
- Take a bucket bath instead of using the shower.
- We can reuse the water left at the dining table for painting, cleaning, mopping and wiping.
- Wastewater from the kitchen can be reused for gardening.
- Rainwater can be collected to water plants or wash cars.

CONCEPT MAP

Water

Sources
- Rain
- Lakes
- Ponds
- Streams
- Seas
- Oceans

Uses
- To live, to grow and to keep bodies healthy
- Drinking
- Bathing
- Washing
- Cooking

Clean drinking water
- Boil water
- Use water filter

Save Water
- Do not leave water taps running
- Take a bucket bath
- Use leftover water for gardening
- Collect and use rainwater

KEYWORDS

Groundwater: rainwater that seeps into the ground

Boil: to heat water to kill germs

Exercise

Objective Type Questions

A. Fill in the blanks.

1. ______________ (Rain/Ocean) is the main source of water.
2. Well is a source of ______________ (clean/underground) water.
3. We use a ______________ (hand pump/water filter) to draw out underground water.
4. It is important to ______________ (strain/purify) drinking water.

B. Write T for True and F for False.

1. Rainwater fills up lakes, rivers and oceans. ◯
2. Boiling makes the water clean. ◯
3. We should throw garbage in lakes and rivers. ◯
4. We can reuse water from our kitchen to water plants. ◯

Subjective Type Questions

Answer the following question.

1. Name any three sources of water.

____

2. What is groundwater?

____

3. Write two ways to purify dirty water.

____

4. Write two ways to keep water clean.

____

5. Write two ways to save water.

____

Application-based Question

Why shouldn't we throw garbage in lakes and rivers?

Picture-based Question

Find the following sources of water in the wordsearch.

R	W	F	N	O	H	N	R
A	M	Z	T	D	A	R	I
I	X	A	A	K	N	P	V
N	N	U	P	V	D	Z	E
K	D	X	E	A	P	W	R
N	S	L	A	K	U	A	M
R	S	N	E	F	M	C	D
W	E	L	L	U	P	X	O

Skill Booster

A. **21CS:** Information literacy | **CC:** Physical Education | **BT:** Psychomotor

Collect pictures of some water games and water activities. Paste these pictures in your scrapbook and write down the names of each. Try playing one of the games.

B. **21CS:** Life Skills | **BT:** Cognitive

Tick (✔) the things we should do and cross (✘) the things we should not do.

- ☐ Drinking water from a roadside tap.
- ☐ Throwing waste in the river.
- ☐ Drinking water from a filter.
- ☐ Keeping a bottle of juice open and drinking from it after 2–3 days.

C. **21CS:** Critical Thinking | **BT:** Cognitive

Imagine a world without water.
How would it affect the following? Fill the table below with your answers.

People	Plants	Animals

Worksheet 4

One day, Thoibi and her family went on a picnic.

'The water is not at all clean, Papa,' complained Thoibi.

'The water carries lots of leaves, branches and fruits of trees that grow on its banks,' Papa replied.

'But Papa, look! There are so many plastic bags, empty packets of chips, empty bottles, all floating in the water!', said Thoibi.

My SEE Journal

A. What were the natural things Thoibi saw floating in the water?

B. What were the man-made things that Thoibi saw floating in the water?

C. Thoibi wanted to take a sip of the river water, but her father stopped her. Why do you think he did so?

My SDG Journal

13 CLIMATE ACTION

A. How did the man-made things come into the river?

B. Why should rivers, lakes and other waterbodies be kept clean?

5 My Needs: Shelter

Prior Knowledge

- Parts of a house
- Need for a house
- Cleanliness of a house

Learning Objectives

- Types of houses
- Types of roofs
- A good and clean house

LET'S GET STARTED

Three little friends live in houses made of three different materials.

Look at the following pictures and guess what their houses are made of.

Choose from the options given in the word box.

bricks	straw	wood

1 ____________ 2 ____________ 3 ____________

Which house do you think is the strongest—the straw house, the brick house or the wooden house? ____________

A house is a place in which we live.

A house protects us from the rain, cold and heat.

A house also protects us from wild animals and thieves.

TYPES OF HOUSES

Look at the pictures given alongside. How is this house similar to or different from your house?

Pucca house

People build different types of houses. Some houses are strong, while some are not so strong.

Some of us live in a city. In cities, houses are mostly made of bricks and cement. Such houses are called ***pucca* houses**. They are strong.

Some of us live in a village. In villages, some houses are made of mud and straw (for example, a hut). Such houses are called ***kutcha* houses**. They are not as strong as *pucca* houses.

Kutcha house

DO YOU KNOW?

In places where it is very cold, houses have heaters to keep them warm. In places where it is very hot, houses are cooled with air conditioners or air coolers to keep them cool.

Permanent Houses

Permanent houses are strong and cannot be moved from one place to another. They are made of cement, bricks, wood and iron. These houses are mostly found in cities and towns.

Some houses have just one storey, for example, cottages and **bungalows**, while some of them are **multi-storeyed**.

WORDS TO KNOW

bungalow: a large house with a lawn

multi-storeyed: having many floors

apartment: a set of rooms in a building to live in

Bungalow

Cottage

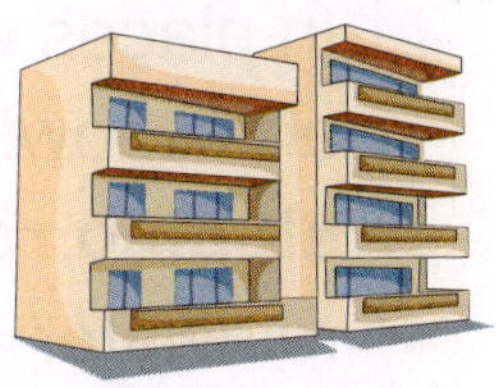

A block of apartments

Temporary Houses

People who keep moving from one place to another often build temporary houses. These houses can be moved from place to place.

Some temporary houses are given below.

Tents are made of **canvas**. They are used by **campers** and soldiers. They can be easily put up, folded and carried along.

Tent

A **caravan** is a house on wheels. People living in caravans can easily move from one place to another.

Caravan

Houseboat

Houseboats are floating houses made of wood. They are found in the lakes of Kashmir and the backwaters of Kerala.

Igloos are houses made of snow. They are found in places that are covered with snow throughout the year.

Igloo

WORDS TO KNOW

canvas: a strong, thick cloth

camper: a person who stays in a tent for a holiday

QUICK REVISION

Fill in the blanks.

1. A ______________ is a house on wheels.
2. A ______________ is made of canvas.
3. Igloos are made of ______________.
4. Houseboats are ______________ houses made of wood.

TYPES OF ROOFS

A roof is found on the top of a house. In different places, houses have different types of roofs.

DO YOU KNOW?

In areas where there is a lot of rainfall, houses are built on **stilts** (wooden poles) above the ground to protect the house from overflowing water.

In places with heavy rainfall and snowfall, houses have **sloping roofs** so that rainwater or snow does not get collected on the roof and can easily slide down.

Sloping roof

In hot areas that do not have much rainfall, houses have **flat roofs**.

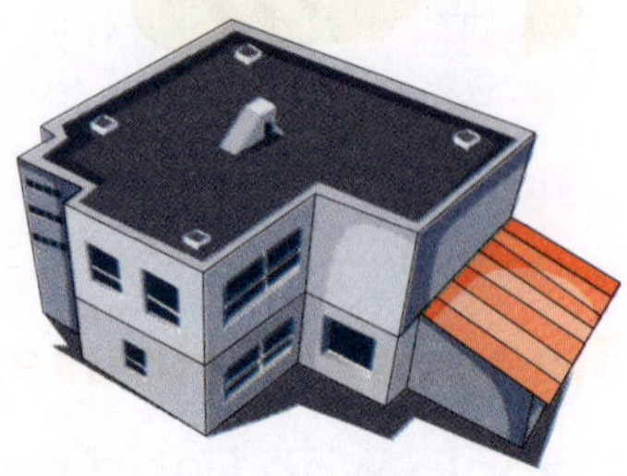

Flat roof

A GOOD AND CLEAN HOUSE

A house must be clean and comfortable. It should be airy.

The area around the house should also be looked after and kept clean.

Given below are some ways to keep a house clean.

A neat and clean house

- We must keep our floors clean by sweeping and mopping them regularly.
- We should keep doors and windows clean and decorate the house with flower pots.
- Kitchen should be kept clean, too, so that the food does not get contaminated with germs.
- We should never scribble on walls.
- The grass in a garden should be mowed, bushes trimmed and flower beds kept neat.

Windows let in sunlight and fresh air

Throwing waste in the bin

- Windows should be kept open to let fresh air and sunlight in.
- Windows should have a wire mesh so that mosquitoes and other insects can be kept out.
- Toilets must be kept clean, too.
- Plants and trees should be planted around the house.

Planting trees and other plants around the house

Taking Care of Our Things

We should take care of the things in our homes. Everyone likes to visit a neat, clean and well-decorated home. We must help at home by keeping our books, toys and clothes in their proper places.

CONCEPT MAP

Types of Houses

Permanent
- Strong houses cannot be moved.
- Made of bricks, cement, wood, iron
- Cottages, bungalows, apartments

Temporary
- Can be moved
- Tents, caravan, houseboats, igloos

Types of Roofs

Sloping Roofs

Areas with heavy rainfall and snowfall

Flat Roofs

In hot areas with less rainfall

KEYWORDS

Pucca house: strong house made of bricks and cement

Kutcha house: house made of mud and straw

Permanent house: house that cannot be moved from place to place

Temporary house: house that can be moved from place to place

Bungalow: one or two storeyed house with a garden

Multi-storyed: house with many floors

Exercise

Objective Type Questions

A. Write T for True and F for False.

1. A house keeps us safe from heat and cold. ◯
2. We can build a permanent house with mud. ◯
3. We find igloos in places that are covered with snow. ◯
4. A flat roof does not let rainwater collect. ◯
5. We should scribble on the walls of our homes. ◯

B. Fill in the blanks.

1. A house ________________ (protects/warms) us from the heat, cold and rain.
2. A *kutcha* house is made of ________________ (bricks/mud).
3. A house should have plenty of ________________ (people/sunlight).
4. In places where there is heavy rainfall and snowfall, houses have ________________ (flat/sloping) roofs.
5. At home, we must keep our things ________________ (scattered/in proper places).

C. Name the following.

1. A mud house ________________
2. A house made of canvas ________________
3. A house on wheels ________________
4. A floating house ________________
5. A house made of snow ________________

Subjective Type Questions

Answer the following questions.

1. Name the materials used to build permanent houses.

____

2. Why do some houses have a sloping roof?

____

3. Make a list of things that you do to keep your house clean.

____

____

Application-based Question

Why do we find so many multi-storeyed buildings in cities?

Picture-based Question

Name the different types of houses shown in the pictures given below.

1. 

____

2. 

____

3. 

____

4. 

____

5. 

____

6. 

____

Skill Booster

A. 21CS: Creativity | CC: Mathematics | AI | BT: Psychomotor

Follow the instructions to make a beautiful paper house.

You will need: Two different-coloured papers, scissors, glue stick and coloured pencils

Method:

1. With the help of an elder, cut out one paper in a square shape and the other paper in a triangle shape.
2. Paste the triangle over the square.
3. Use the coloured pencils to draw the door and windows.

Your paper house is ready!

B. 21CS: Life Skills | BT: Cognitive, Affective

Tick (✔) the things you would do to help keep your house clean.

- ☐ Make your bed after you get up in the morning.
- ☐ Throw waste all around the house.
- ☐ Fill your water bottle for school.
- ☐ Splash water all over the bathroom.
- ☐ Pick up your plate after finishing your meal and put it in the sink for washing.
- ☐ Walk into the house with muddy shoes.
- ☐ Pick up your toys after playing and keep them back in the toy box.

What can you do to keep your classroom clean? Get into groups with the help of your teacher. Now, take turns in keeping your classroom clean.

Worksheet 5

Every morning, Pritha's mother opens all the windows in the house and draws the curtains to the sides. As a result, the whole house gets lit up by sunlight. Pritha loves standing at the open windows and gazing at the world outside.

My SEE Journal

A. What can Pritha do to keep her room airy?

____

____

____

____

____

____

____

B. How do you help at home by taking care of your room?

____

____

____

____

____

____

My SDG Journal

3 GOOD HEALTH AND WELL-BEING

A. Why does Pritha's mother shut the window at night?

____

____

____

____

____

____

B. Why is it important for our rooms to get fresh air and sunlight?

____

____

____

____

____

____

6 My Needs: Clothing

Prior Knowledge
- Need for clothes
- Variety of clothes
- Care of clothes

Learning Objectives
- Clothes for different seasons
- Natural and man-made fibres

LET'S GET STARTED

Jerry, Menka and Hiyang have dressed up to go to different places. Can you guess where they are going? Match the pictures with the words given below.

Jerry

Menka

Hiyang

Swimming   School   Picnic

NEED FOR CLOTHES

We wear clothes to protect our body from the heat, rain and cold. Clothes also make us look smart.

We wear a uniform to school. Some grown ups also wear uniform when they go to work. We wear special clothes for special occasions.

We also wear different kinds of clothes for different seasons.

- **Summer season**: It is very hot during summer. We wear light-coloured **cotton** clothes because they keep our body cool.
- **Rainy season**: During the rainy season, we wear raincoats and gumboots. We also carry umbrellas to keep ourselves dry.
- **Winter season**: It is cold during the winter season. To keep ourselves warm, we wear thick and heavy **woollen** clothes. We may use a muffler and gloves during this cold season. We also wear clothes made of silk material.

In very cold places, people wear clothes made of fur.

Summer clothes

WORD TO KNOW

fur: soft, thick body hair of some animals

Clothes for rainy season

Winter clothes

DO YOU KNOW?

Early humans used to cover their bodies with leaves, barks of trees and even animal skin!

QUICK REVISION

Fill in the blanks.

1. Clothes make us look ____________.
2. We wear light ____________ clothes during summer.
3. We wear a ____________ on a rainy day.

NATURAL AND MAN-MADE FIBRES

Look at your shirt/skirt/socks/pants. What are these made of? These clothes are made up of fibres.

Fibres are thread-like materials that are woven together to make fabric.

Natural Fibres

Fibres that come from plants and animals are called **natural fibres**.

Plant Fibres

Some of the fibre that comes from plants are given below.

- **Cotton:** Cotton comes from cotton plants. It is used to make light, summer clothes.
- **Jute:** Jute comes from jute plants. It is used to make bags, ropes and mats.

Jute bag Cotton frock

Things made from plant fibres

Animal Fibres

Some of the fibre that we get from animals are given below.

- **Wool:** The hair of sheep or yak is woven to make wool. Wool is used to make sweaters and other warm clothes.
- **Silk:** We get silk from silkworms. They build a cocoon around themselves and we get silk thread from this cocoon. The thread is then woven to form silk.
- **Fur:** Fur is the soft hair on the body of some animals. In very cold places, people wear clothes made of fur.

Silk sari Woollen sweater

Things made from animal fibres

Artificial Fibres

Artificial fibres are made by human beings. Nylon, rayon, polyester and terylene are examples of artificial fibres.

CARE OF DIFFERENT TYPES OF CLOTHES

Some ways of taking care of clothes are given below.

- The cotton uniform you wear to school must be washed every day.
- Coats and jackets have to be dry-cleaned.

- Silk clothes need a gentle wash or have to be dry-cleaned.
- Woollen clothes have to be washed or dry-cleaned and put away with naphthalene balls after the winter season. In cold countries, we need to wear woollen clothes throughout the year.

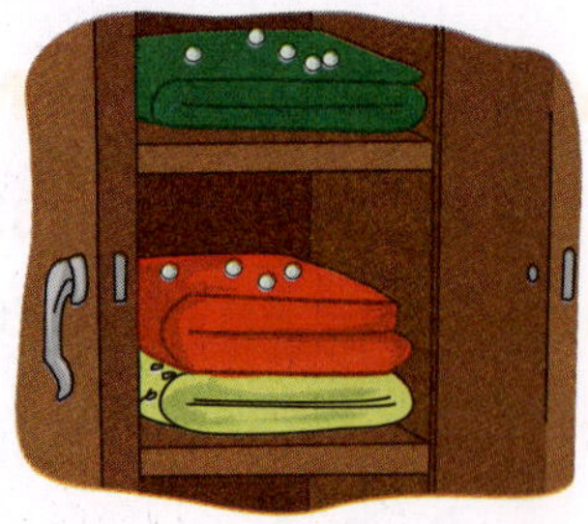

Naphthalene balls kept between clothes

CONCEPT MAP

Types of Clothes

- **Summer**: Light-coloured cotton clothes
- **Rainy Season**: Raincoat and gumboots
- **Winter**: Thick, heavy woollen clothes

Fibres

Thread-like materials that are woven together to make fabric

- **Plant Fibre**
  - Cotton
  - Jute
- **Animal Fibre**
  - Wool
  - Fur
  - Silk

KEYWORDS

Cotton: type of light, soft fabric

Woollen: made out of wool

Fibre: thread-like materials that are woven together to make fabric

Natural fibre: fibres that come from plants or animals

Artificial fibres: fibres that are made by humans

Exercise

Objective Type Questions

A. Choose the correct answer.

1. ______________ clothes keep us cool in summer.

   a. Silk b. Linen c. Cotton d. Fur

2. These clothes have to be dry-cleaned.

   a. Coats b. Socks c. Vests d. Ties

3. ______________ is a type of man-made fibre.

   a. Jute b. Silk c. Nylon d. Cotton

4. In very cold places, people wear clothes made of ______________ .

   a. fur b. silk c. cotton d. nylon

B. Fill in the blanks.

1. ______________ (Uniform/Sweaters) must be washed every day.
2. ______________ (Woollen/Coats) clothes must be washed separately.
3. Silk is made by ______________ (glow-worms/silkworms).
4. Polyester is ______________ (a natural/an artificial) fibre.

Subjective Type Questions

Answer the following questions.

1. What kind of clothes do we wear during the winter season?

   ____

2. What are fibres?

   ____

3. Name the different kinds of fibres. Give examples.

   ____

4. Write down three ways to take care of our clothes.

   ____

Application-based Question

Rajni is going to a hill station during her winter vacation. What kind of clothes should she pack to keep herself warm?

Picture-based Question

Read the names of clothes given below. Write them down in the correct column.

To be washed at home	To be dry-cleaned

Skill Booster

A. **21CS:** Information Literacy | **CC:** Social Studies | **BT:** Cognitive, Affective

With the help of an adult, collect pictures of the traditional dresses of the people from four different countries and paste them in your scrapbook. Do not forget to write down the name of the country, the name of the dress and the name of the material it is made of.

B. **21CS:** Creativity and Innovation | **AI** | **CC:** Mathematics | **BT:** Psychomotor

You will need two rolls of a narrow satin ribbon, a thick old cardboard piece and some board pins.

Note: Take help of your teacher to do this.

1. Cut thin strips of both the satin ribbons.
2. Fix one set of ribbons on the cardboard lengthwise, as shown in Fig. 2.
3. Now, take the other ribbon and place it over the first ribbon that is fixed lengthwise on the cardboard.
4. Then, pass it under the second and again over the third, and so on until you reach the other side of the cardboard, as shown in Fig. 3.
5. Repeat with all other ribbons until a mat-like pattern is made.
6. Laminating will protect your mat.

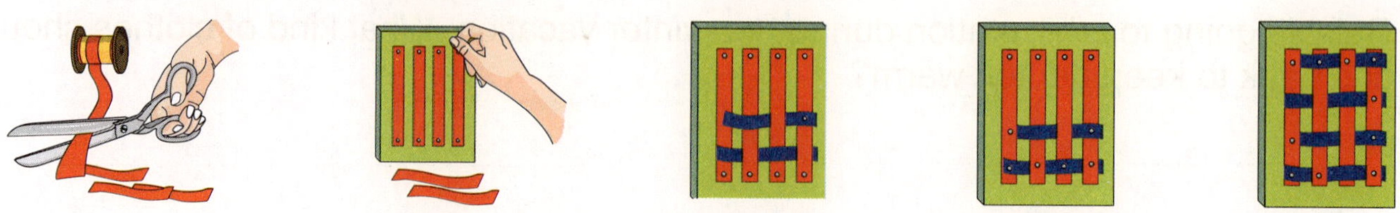

① ② ③ ④ ⑤

Worksheet 6

My SEE Journal

A. Why did Rajiv need winter clothing?

B. Why could Rajiv not wear last year's clothes?

My SDG Journal

12 RESPONSIBLE CONSUMPTION AND PRODUCTION

A. What can Rajiv do with his old clothes?

B. What do you do with the clothes, books and toys that you no longer need?

C. Why is it good to give things we no longer need to the children who need them?

7 My Needs: Air

Prior Knowledge

- Air all around us
- Need for clean air
- Plants help clean the air

Learning Objectives

- Properties of air
- What makes air dirty
- How to keep air clean
- Airborne diseases and their prevention

LET'S GET STARTED

You must have seen people blowing balloons for birthday parties.

1. What do we blow into the balloon?

____

2. Can you see what is inside the balloon?

____

3. How do you know that it is inside?

____

AIR AROUND US

Air is all around us. We cannot see air but can feel it. We feel air when we switch on the fan.

When air moves, the leaves on trees sway. Moving air is called **wind**. A gentle wind is called a **breeze**.

Strong wind is called a **storm**. It may uproot trees or damage buildings.

Breeze

Storm

What is a gale?

FIND OUT

PROPERTIES OF AIR

You have already learnt that air has no colour and clean air has no smell. Let us learn about some more properties of air through some activities.

DO IT YOURSELF

1. Take a balloon and blow air into it. You will see that the balloon grows in size.

   What is in the balloon?

   It is air.

   So, we can say air fills up space.

2. Look at the picture given below.

   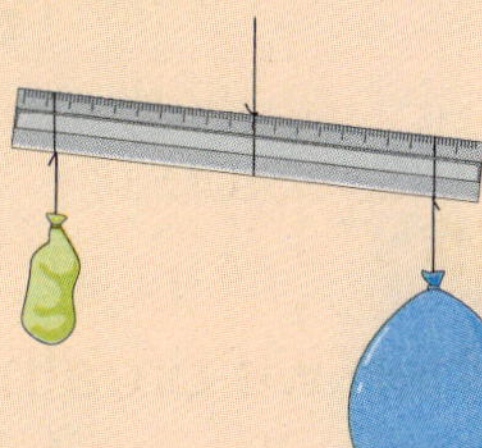

   Why do you think the scale is tilted towards the side with the blown-up balloon?

   This is because air has weight.

DO YOU KNOW?

We cannot live on the moon because the moon does not have air!

QUICK REVISION

Write T for True and F for False.

1. A strong wind is called breeze. ◯
2. A gentle wind is called storm. ◯
3. Air takes up space. ◯

WHAT MAKES AIR DIRTY

Smoke released from chimneys, cars, factories and from burning things makes the air dirty. Dust and germs also make it unfit for breathing.

Smoke from vehicles, factories and burning wood makes the air dirty

DO YOU KNOW?

Germs in the air make us fall ill.

FIND OUT

Why should you cover your mouth when you sneeze?

CLEAN AIR

We should always breathe in fresh and clean air. Fresh air keeps us healthy.

Plants make the air fresh by producing oxygen. This is why we should plant more trees. We should cycle to short distances instead of using a car. Factories must filter harmful gases before releasing them from their chimneys.

We must not burn leaves, paper, wood or crackers as it makes the air dirty.

Plant trees

Cycle to short distances

Do not burn things

AIRBORNE DISEASES

Diseases that spread when we breathe in dirty air are called airborne diseases. Some examples of airborne diseases are given below.

- Asthma
- Cold and cough
- Chickenpox
- Measles

Prevention of Airborne Diseases

To prevent airborne diseases from spreading, we should take the following steps.

- Cover your mouth while coughing or sneezing.
- Wear a mask if you go to a place where the air is dirty or if you are suffering from an airborne infection (example: COVID-19).
- If you are suffering from an airborne disease, stay home and rest so that you do not spread the disease.

Cover your mouth while coughing or sneezing

CONCEPT MAP

Air

Moving air: wind

Gentle wind: breeze

Strong wind: storm

Properties:

- No colour
- No smell

What makes air dirty

- Smoke
- Dust
- Germs

Keep air clean

- Plant more trees
- Avoid using cars
- Factories must filter harmful gases
- Do not burn leaves, paper, wood, crackers

KEYWORDS

Wind: moving air

Breeze: gentle wind

Storm: strong wind

Airborne diseases: diseases spread by breathing in air that has germs

Exercise

Objective Type Questions

A. Fill in the blanks.

1. Moving air is called ____________ (steam/wind).
2. Air is needed for ____________ (writing/burning).
3. Germs in the air make the air ____________ (fit/unfit) for breathing.
4. Plants help in keeping the air clean by producing ____________ (carbon dioxide/oxygen).

B. Correct the sentences.

1. We can see air in a balloon.

   ____

2. A gentle wind is called storm.

   ____

Subjective Type Questions

Answer the following questions.

1. Write any two uses of air.

   ____

   ____

2. What makes the air dirty?

   ____

   ____

Application-based Question

Neil Armstrong was the first man to land on the moon. Why do you think he carried a tank of air when he went there?

Picture-based Question

Which of the following is good for the air around us? Put a tick (✔) mark.

 ○  ○  ○  ○

Skill Booster

A. 21CS: Creativity and Innovation | AI | CC: Mathematics | BT: Psychomotor

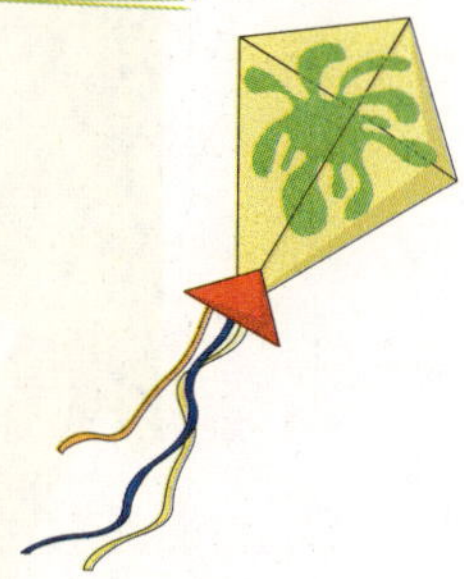

Make your own kite!

You will need: Thin kite paper (cut in a diamond shape), liquid paint, paper ribbons

Method: Put a blob of paint on the kite paper and blow over it to spread it on the kite. Continue doing this to make a design. Keep it aside to dry. Cut out paper ribbons and attach them to the tail of the kite. Your paper kite is ready!

B. 21CS: Life Skills | BT: Cognitive, Affective

Grow a plant in your garden or keep a potted plant in your balcony or in your windowsill. Water it regularly. Take a picture of your plant, paste it in your scrapbook and write how you take care of it.

C. 21CS: Critical Thinking, Creativity and Innovation | AI | BT: Affective, Psychomotor

When we cut trees, we are actually harming ourselves. Create a poster to show how the cutting of trees is harmful to us.

Worksheet 7

Sheila and Rama had come on a vacation with their families to a remote village

My SEE Journal

A. Why was the air cleaner in the mountain village?

____

____

____

____

B. Why did they think they would be healthier while living there?

____

____

____

____

____

My SDG Journal

13 CLIMATE ACTION

A. What makes the air around us dirty?

____

____

____

____

B. In what ways can you change your habits to have cleaner air in the world you live in?

____

____

____

____

8 Staying Clean, Healthy and Safe

Prior Knowledge

- Personal hygiene
- Cleanliness in the house and surroundings
- Use of dustbin in the house/school
- Safety at home and outside

Learning Objectives

- Ways to keep ourselves clean
- Exercise and rest
- How to avoid falling sick
- Safety rules
- First aid

LET'S GET STARTED

Which room would you like to stay in? Tick (✔) your choice. Give reasons for your answer.

1  ◯

2  ◯

A POEM!

Sing this song in the tune of '*If you are happy and you know it*' along with actions.

If you are clean and you know it,
brush your teeth.

If you are clean and you know it
and you really want to show it,

If you are clean and you know it,
brush your teeth.

Now, sing again by changing the words written in orange with different actions.

KEEPING OURSELVES CLEAN

In Class 1, we have learnt about the ways to keep ourselves clean. Let us revise them.

Brush your teeth twice a day

Take a bath every day

Wear clean clothes

Clip your nails regularly

Comb your hair neatly

Staying clean keeps you healthy and protects you from falling sick.

QUICK REVISION

Write good or bad for each of the following sentences.

1. I will bathe every day. __________
2. I will not brush my teeth every day. __________
3. I will cut my nails only after they grow very long. __________
4. I will comb my hair only once a week. __________

CLEAN SURROUNDINGS

We know that it is important to keep our surroundings clean. Clean surroundings keep us healthy by not letting disease-causing germs to grow.

It is our duty to look after our surroundings and keep them clean.

Ways to Keep Our Surroundings Clean

Some ways to keep our surroundings clean are given below.

- Do not throw trash on the road or on footpath. Throw garbage in a bin or wait for the garbage collector to come and take it.

Throwing waste in a bin

- While throwing garbage, one should sort out the trash and throw it in their proper bins.

Sorting and throwing waste into proper bins

- Parks are places visited by many children and adults. They should be kept litter-free. Dustbins should be kept for throwing trash.
- It is important for people to keep their houses clean too. An unclean house does not look nice. Garbage should be cleared regularly.
- We should also keep our school clean. Throw waste paper and pencil shavings in a dustbin.

EXERCISE AND REST

To stay fit, we need to exercise regularly.

Some forms of exercise are given below.

TALK TIME

What do you like to do in your free time?

Playing

Running

Skipping

Cycling

Yoga

Rest is also very important for our body. We must relax and sleep well after a hard day's work! We need to sleep for 7 to 8 hours every day. Our mind also needs rest. In order to relax and feel fresh, we can do various activities, such as listening to music, reading a book or playing indoor games.

HOW TO AVOID FALLING SICK

Sometimes, we fall sick. Then, we must visit a doctor. A doctor gives us medicines to help us feel better. We can avoid falling sick by doing the following.

- Eat healthy food.
- Exercise regularly.
- Keep ourselves clean.
- Throw waste only in dustbins.
- Drink plenty of water.
- Take enough rest.
- Keep our surroundings clean.

SAFETY RULES

The rules we follow to keep ourselves safe from accidents are called **safety rules**.

SAFETY RULES AT HOME

- Do not play with sharp objects such as scissors, knives or forks. You might hurt yourself.
- Do not touch an electric wire or a switch with wet hands. You might get an electric shock.
- Do not splash soapy water on the bathroom floor. Someone might slip and fall.
- Do not go near a hot iron or touch a hot pot or a stove that is lit. You might get burnt.
- Put your toys back in their place after playing. Otherwise, somebody might trip over them.
- Do not climb on balcony walls. You might fall and hurt yourself.
- Do not play with matches. You might get burnt.
- Never take or give medicines without asking an elder.

SAFETY RULES IN THE PLAYGROUND

- Always play a safe game and do not push others.
- Wait for your turn on slides and swings. Do not stand in front of a swing.
- Never play near thorny bushes or **barbed** wires.
- While running, be **alert** and keep your eyes open, so that you do not bump into others.
- Never go for a swim alone. Always swim with an elder.
- Do not tease **stray** animals. They might bite you.

WORD TO KNOW

barbed: having a pointed end

alert: careful

stray: an animal that is homeless

SAFETY RULES ON THE ROAD

- Never play on the road.
- Always walk on the footpath.
- Cross the road at a zebra crossing.
- Cross the road only when the **pedestrian** light turns green.
- Before crossing the road, look to your right, left and then right again.
- Cross the road only when the road is clear.
- Do not talk to strangers.

SAFETY RULES IN A VEHICLE

- Always wear a seatbelt when sitting inside a car.
- Never stand in a moving car or bus.
- Always wait for the bus to stop before getting into or getting off it.
- Never put your hand or head out of a moving vehicle. A passing vehicle might hurt you.
- Do not shout at or disturb the person driving a car or bus.

QUICK REVISION

Write T for true and F for false.

1. We should play with sharp objects. ◯
2. We should walk on the footpath. ◯
3. We should cross the road at a zebra crossing. ◯
4. We must wear a seatbelt when sitting in a car. ◯
5. We should tease stray animals. ◯

GOOD TOUCH AND BAD TOUCH

Some touches make you feel safe and happy. These are **good touches**. Some touches make you feel unsafe and uncomfortable. These are **bad touches**.

Table 8.1 Good and bad touches

Good Touch	Bad Touch
When your parents hug you	When someone touches you where you do not want to be touched
When your parents give you a goodnight kiss	When a person touches you under your clothes
When your friend hugs and kisses you	A touch that makes you feel scared

FIRST AID

Sometimes, accidents happen even when you are careful. In such situations, the people around must help the person who is hurt. If someone around you gets hurt, then call an elder.

The help given to a person who is hurt before the doctor comes is called **first aid**.

CONCEPT MAP

Keeping Youself Clean and Healthy

- Brush your teeth
- Take a bath
- Wear clean clothes
- Comb your hair
- Exercise and rest
- Clip your nails

Keep Your Surroundings Clean

- Do not throw trash on the road
- Sort out trash and throw in proper bins
- Keep parks litter-free
- Keep your school clean

Keeping Safe

At home

- Do not play with sharp objects
- Do not touch electric wire with wet hands
- Do not splash soapy water
- Do not go near a hot iron or a hot stove
- Put your toys back after playing
- Do not climb on the balcony walls

In School

- Do not run around
- Always walk in a queue
- Be careful while going up and down the stairs
- Do not stand or jump off desks and chairs

In the Playground

- Play a safe game
- Wait for your turn
- Avoid thorny bushes or barbed wires
- Be alert and do not bump into others

In a vehicle

- Wear a seatbelt
- Do not stand in a moving bus or car
- Wait for the bus to stop
- Do not put your hand or head out
- Do not shout

On the road

- Do not play on the road
- Walk on the footpath
- Cross at zebra crossing
- Cross when the pedestrian light is green and check if the road is clear

KEYWORDS

Safety rules: the rules we follow to keep ourselves safe from accidents

Good touches: some touches that make you feel safe and happy

Bad touches: some touches that make you feel unsafe and uncomfortable

First aid: help given to a person who is hurt before the doctor comes

Exercise

Objective Type Questions

A. Fill in the blanks.

1. We must ________ (rinse/brush) our teeth twice a day.
2. ________ (Cycling/Sleeping) is a form of exercise that keeps us fit.
3. Never play with sharp objects such as ________ (knife/spoon) and ________ (scissors/dolls).
4. Cross the road only when the pedestrian light is ________ (red/green).
5. The help given to someone who is hurt before the doctor comes is called ________ (last aid/first aid).

B. Write T for True and F for False.

1. We must take a bath every week. ◯
2. We should keep our surroundings clean to be healthy. ◯
3. Regular exercise keeps our body fit. ◯
4. We should sleep for only 2 hours a day. ◯
5. Do not stand in front of a swing in the playground. ◯
6. Before crossing the road, look to your right, left and then right again. ◯
7. Always cross the road at a zebra crossing. ◯

C. Match the following.

1. Teeth	a. Electric shock
2. Hair	b. Sleep
3. Exercise	c. For crossing the road
4. Rest	d. Skipping
5. Safety rules	e. Comb
6. Electric wire	f. People walking on the road
7. Pedestrians	g. Toothbrush
8. Zebra crossing	h. Prevent accidents

Subjective Type Questions

Answer the following questions.

1. Name any two exercises that keep us fit.

____

2. Write any two ways to avoid falling sick.

____

3. What is first aid?

____

4. Write some ways to keep your surroundings clean.

____

____

5. Write any three safety rules to be followed at school.

____

____

6. Why should you not put your hand out of a moving bus?

____

____

Application-based Questions

A. If you have a toothache, who will you go to?

B. Anjali always tries to switch on the burner of the gas stove when her mother is not at home. Is it safe to do so?

Picture-based Question

Look at the picture given below. Three children in the picture are not following the safety rules. Circle those three children.

Skill Booster

A. **21CS:** Communication, Life Skills | **BT:** Cognitive, Affective

Nobody likes to play with Aditya because he has bad breath. He comes to school without brushing his teeth. As a friend, what should you do? Tick (✔) the correct option.

☐ Avoid playing with him.

☐ Ask him to brush his teeth twice a day.

☐ Ask him not to come to school.

B. **21CS:** Collaboration, Creativity and Innovation | AI | **BT:** Affective, Psychomotor

Divide the class into five groups. Ask each group to make posters using chart paper and crayons on the safety rules that are to be followed:

a. in the classroom b. in the playground c. in a vehicle

d. on the road e. at home

C. **21CS:** Critical Thinking | **BT:** Cognitive, Affective

You and your mother are walking on a road when suddenly her phone begins to ring. What should you do? Tick (✔) the correct option.

☐ Wait for her to finish the call.

☐ Pull her to cross the road.

☐ Leave her standing to finish the call and keep walking by yourself.

D. **21CS:** Creativity and Innovation, Life Skills | AI | **CC:** English | **BT:** Affective, Psychomotor

Recreate these paper puppets. With the help of an elder, cut out the puppets with scissors. Wrap each one around your fingers as shown. Fasten the open ends with glue one by one.

Now, use these finger puppets to tell a story about good and bad touches.

Worksheet 8

Every morning, at around seven o'clock, garbage collectors would come around, blowing their whistle. Debnath would watch from his upstairs window, as, hearing the whistle, people would come out of the neighbouring houses and deposit trash into the carts. Each person would bring two bags and deposit one each in the two carts.

My SEE Journal

A. How clean do you think Debnath's neighbourhood is? Why do you think so?

B. Why do people carry two bags of garbage to deposit in two different carts?

My SDG Journal

13 CLIMATE ACTION

A. Why is it necessary for us to hand over the garbage to a collector rather than throw it on the street?

B. What would you tell someone who throws garbage on the road?

9 Places in the Neighbourhood

Prior Knowledge

- Our neighbours
- Our neighbourhood
- People in our neighbourhood

Learning Objectives

- Places in our neighbourhood
- People who help us
- Emergency vehicles
- Fun places in the neighbourhood

LET'S GET STARTED

Ritam has just moved into a new house and does not know his way home well. Help him find the way to his house.

NEIGHBOURHOOD

The area around our house is known as our **neighbourhood**. Many people live in our neighbourhood. They are our **neighbours**.

TALK TIME

- Name two of your friends who live in your neighbourhood.
- How do you spend time with them?

GOOD NEIGHBOURS

- Good neighbours help each other and are friends with one another.
- Good neighbours never fight with one another.
- Good neighbours celebrate festivals together.

PLACES IN OUR NEIGHBOURHOOD

A good neighbourhood should have all the important places closeby.

- **Market:** Local markets sell items of daily needs such as fresh fruits and vegetables, fresh flowers, animal products and milk products. In big cities, there are shopping malls in almost every area.

- **Hospital/Clinic:** It is important to have a hospital or a clinic nearby in case people fall sick. Doctors and nurses look after us in a hospital or clinic.

- **School:** A school in the neighbourhood helps children by teaching them how to read and write. The teachers also help children to draw, colour, play, sing and dance.

- **Police Station:** Police officers protect us and our neighbourhood. They keep a watch over our neighbourhood and keep us safe from robbers and thieves.

- **Fire Station:** Fire stations have trained firefighters who can come and help in case a fire starts in our neighbourhood.

- **Bank:** People keep their money in a bank for safety and take it out only when they need it. The banks also have lockers where people can keep their jewellery and other important papers.

- **Park:** It is important for all neighbourhoods to have a park, as it is a place where children play and adults may walk or jog or simply sit and talk to their friends.

- **Post Office:** We can send letters and parcels from a post office. Postmen come to collect and deliver letters every day.

- **Petrol Pump:** Petrol pumps are the places where people go to fill petrol or diesel for their cars. Some petrol pumps have mechanics who repair vehicles as well.

- **Bus Stop:** A good neighbourhood also has a bus stop or two where buses stop to pick up or drop passengers.

Name a market place or a shopping mall that is close to your house. **FIND OUT**

QUICK REVISION

Name the following.

1. Place where we keep our money safe ________________
2. Place where we go when we do not feel well ________________
3. Place where we call in case of a fire ________________

PEOPLE WHO HELP US

We have many other people who help us in our daily lives. Some of them are given below.

- **Electrician:** A person who looks after the electrical connections in our house.
- **Mason**: A person who works with stones, bricks and cement, etc. to build a house.
- **Courier serviceman:** A person who delivers parcels or letters sent through a courier service.
- **Gas serviceman:** A person who comes home to check and repair gas stoves.

We should be thankful to and respect all those people who make our lives comfortable. Remember, all kinds of jobs are important in their own way.

Who is a chemist? **FIND OUT**

EMERGENCIES

In times of emergencies, neighbours always help each other. However sometimes, we need others to come to our rescue.

Make a note of the following telephone numbers and keep it next to your telephone.

- Police
- Fire brigade
- Ambulance
- Gas repair service centre

FUN PLACES IN THE NEIGHBOURHOOD

Everybody needs some time for fun, especially during weekends. Thus, they like to go to a cinema, park, or even to a mall to have fun. They also visit their neighbours and have fun together with their friends.

It is important for us to keep our neighbourhood clean. We must never disturb our neighbours by playing loud music or watching the television at a high volume. Being helpful, respectful and kind will make us good neighbours.

CONCEPT MAP

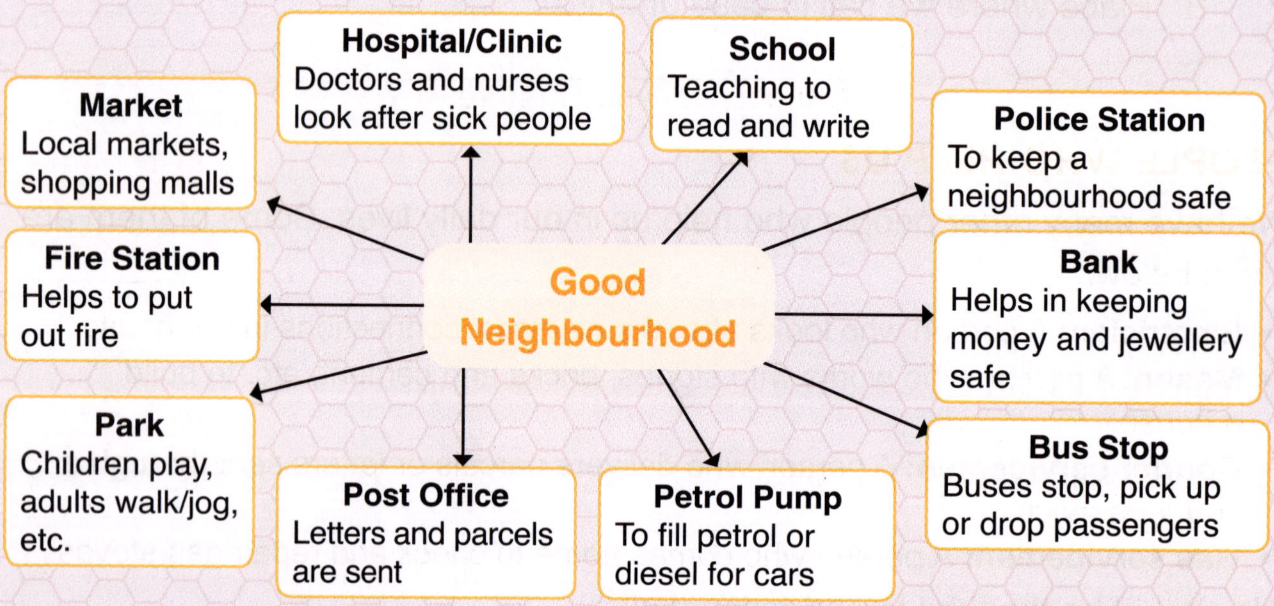

KEYWORDS

Neighbourhood: the area around our house

Neighbours: the people who live in our neighbourhood

Clinic: a place where sick people are treated

Bank: a place to keep your money and jewellery safe

Exercise

Objective Type Questions

A. Fill in the blanks.

1. The ______________ (city/area) in which you live is your neighbourhood.
2. Banks have ______________ (accounts/lockers) to keep our jewellery safe.
3. A ______________ (plumber/electrician) repairs our plugs and switches.
4. It is our duty to keep our neighbourhood ______________ (clean/unclean).

B. Name the following.

1. A place you go to report a robbery ______________
2. A person who looks after the electrical connections in our house ______________
3. He repairs our gas stoves ______________
4. A courier service man delivers this ______________

Subjective Type Questions

Answer the following questions.

1. Who are our neighbours?

____

____

2. How is a policeman helpful?

____

____

3. What do good neighbours do?

____

____

4. Why is it important to have a hospital in the neighbourhood?

____

____

Application-based Question

Your neighbour has gone on a holiday. When you look out of the window, you see a strange-looking man entering his/her house. What should you do?

Picture-based Question

Name the places given below. Match the following places with their descriptions.

People keep their money at this place for safety and take it out when they need it.

We can send letters and parcels from this place.

Doctors and nurses look after us when we fall sick at this place.

Skill Booster

A. **21CS:** Information Literacy **BT:** Cognitive, Affective

Find out the names of at least ten people who help us live our lives comfortably.

B. **21CS:** Life Skills **BT:** Cognitive, Affective

Your friend's mother who lives next door is unwell. How can you help your friend and his mother? Put a tick (✔) or a cross (✘).

☐ Ask your mother to send some medicines for the sick person.

☐ Take her to the hospital.

☐ Help your friend by doing homework together.

☐ Play music loudly.

C. **21CS:** Critical Thinking **BT:** Affective

A plumber was called to repair the leaking taps and pipes in your home. He worked all day. He was very tired by the end of the day. What would you do? Tick (✔) the correct action.

☐ Offer him a cup of tea or a glass of water.

☐ Talk to him rudely and ask him to finish his work quickly.

☐ Scold him for doing his job very slowly.

Worksheet 9

'Priya, it's Sunday today. I have a few things to buy from the market. Would you like to come with me?' asked Priya's mother.

'Let's go, Mama. Let me bring two shopping bags. We both can carry one each.'

'That's good thinking, Priya. I will let you carry the lighter items. Shall we walk to the market?'

'Let's walk. It will be good exercise. The market is not too far away.'

My SEE Journal

A. Why are Priya and her mother carrying bags when shops usually give goods in plastic bags?

____

____

____

____

____

B. Why is Priya carrying a bag as well?

____

____

____

____

____

My SDG Journal

13 CLIMATE ACTION

A. How does Priya and her mother show that they care for the environment?

____

____

____

B. Why is plastic not good for the world we live in?

____

____

____

C. What can you do to reduce the use of plastic?

____

____

10 Plants

Prior Knowledge
- Big and small plants
- Food and medicines from plants
- Places where plants grow

Learning Objectives
- Types of plants
- Parts of a plant
- How plants are useful to us

LET'S GET STARTED

Trees are home to many birds and animals.

Name four animals or birds that live on trees. Draw any two animals or birds that you named near the tree.

____

Plants are found everywhere. They grow on land and in water.

PLANTS THAT GROW ON LAND

In Class 1, we learnt about the different types of plants. Let us revise.

A tree

TALK TIME

Name the following trees.

Trees

Big plants are called **trees**. They are strong plants. They have thick stems called trunks.

Shrubs

Some plants are small and have many branches. They are called **shrubs**. For example, rose, *tulsi* and *Hibiscus*.

Tulsi

Rose

Herbs

Some plants are very small and have soft, weak and green stems. They are called **herbs**. For example, grass and mint.

Grass

Climbers

Plants with weak stems that need support to grow are called **climbers**. For example, money plant and grapevine.

Money plant

Creepers

Plants with very weak stems that creep on the ground are called **creepers**. For example, watermelon and pumpkin plant.

Pumpkin plant

PLANTS THAT GROW IN WATER

Some water plants include water lily, water chestnut, lotus and duckweed. Plants such as lotus and water lily have floating leaves. Some plants grow completely underwater, such as *Hydrilla*.

Water lily

DO YOU KNOW?

- Potatoes, onions and ginger are the stems that grow underground.
- A cactus plant has leaves turned into thorns or spines. The fleshy green part that you see is actually the stem.
- Banyan trees have their roots growing from the branches downwards. They are called prop roots, as they support the heavy branches of the trees.
- The peanut plant has flowers above the ground, but the peanuts grow underground.

PARTS OF A PLANT

A plant has different parts. Let us learn about them.

Leaves make food for the plant.

Flowers help in producing fruits.

Fruits have **seeds** inside them.

New plants grow from seeds.

Stem carries water and food to all parts of the plant.

Roots hold the plant to the ground. Roots also take in water for the plant from the soil.

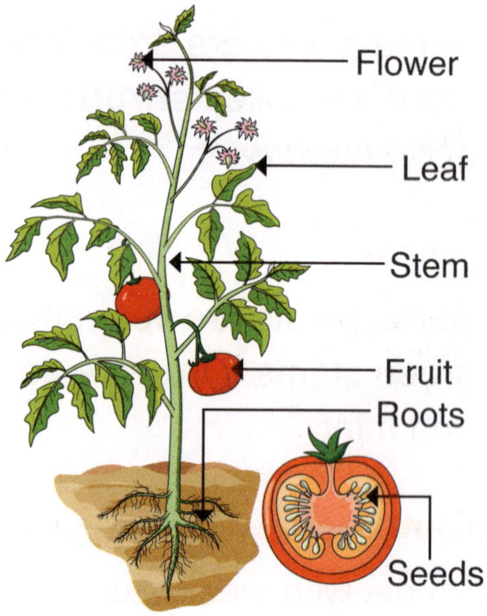

Parts of a plant

QUICK REVISION

Match the following.

1. Root	a. Make food for the plant
2. Stem	b. Produces fruit
3. Flower	c. Holds the plant to the ground
4. Leaves	d. Carries water to all parts of the plant

USEFUL PLANTS

Plants not only make the Earth beautiful but are also very useful to us. Most of the food we eat comes from plants. We eat different parts of a plant.

These are some **leaves** that we eat.

Cabbage

Spinach

Coriander

DO YOU KNOW?

To make our food tasty, we add spices such as pepper, cardamom, coriander seeds and cinnamon (bark of a tree).

Cardamom

These are some **roots** that we eat.

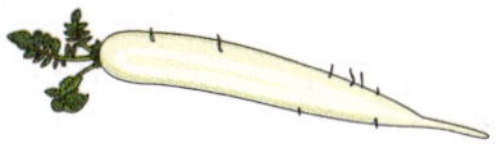
Radish

Turnip

Carrots

These are some **stems** that we eat.

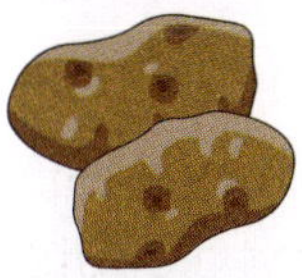
Potatoes

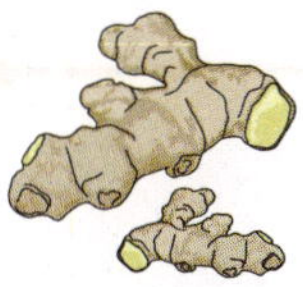
Ginger

Sugarcane

These are some **seeds** that we eat.

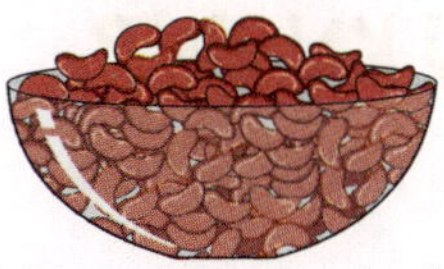
Kidney beans (rajma)

Rice

Wheat

These are some **fruits** that we eat.

Guava

Mango

Orange

Strawberry

Apple

We need **oil** for cooking. Cooking oil is made by crushing the seeds of the plants.

Groundnut oil

Sunflower oil

Mustard oil

Many medicines are made from plants such as *tulsi,* neem, mint, cloves and aloe vera.

Mint leaves

Cloves

Aloe vera

FIND OUT

What do we call coriander and cumin seeds in Hindi, Urdu, Tamil, Assamese, Bengali, Gujarati, Marathi and Malayalam?

The cotton plant gives us the fibre that is woven into fabric to make clothes. The jute plant gives us the fibre that is woven into jute cloth that is then used for making bags, mats and even clothes.

Jute plant

Jute bag

Cotton plant

Cotton dress

Paper is made from the wood of trees and plants such as the bamboo plant.

Bamboo plant

Paper

DO YOU KNOW?

Bamboo is the tallest grass.

The rubber tree gives us rubber. It is used to make tyres, shoes, gloves, pipes and erasers.

Rubber tree

Tyre

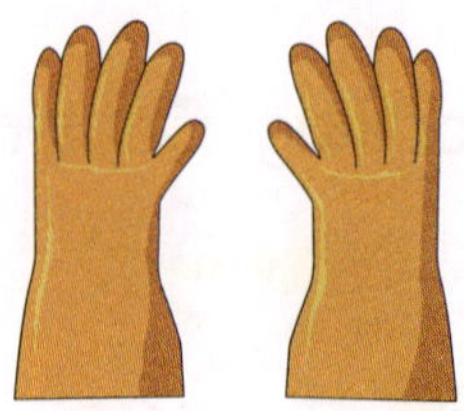

Gloves

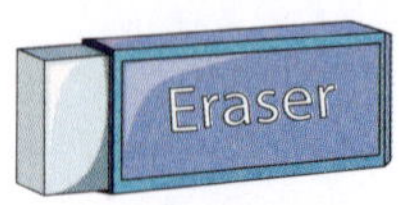

Eraser

Perfumes are made from flowers such as rose and jasmine.

Perfume from rose flowers

Bird's nest

Monkey sitting on a tree

Trees and plants are homes to a variety of animals, birds and insects.

Wood from trees such as teak and pine is used to make furniture such as tables and chairs.

Chair and table made from wood

CARE OF PLANTS

- Like us, plants also need water. So, we must water the plants regularly.
- Plants need sunlight to make food. So, we must put our potted plants in places where they can receive the warmth of the sun.
- We should not pluck leaves and flowers from plants.
- We should not cut trees.

Friends With a Tree

Go on a nature walk. Choose a tree and make friends with it.

What tree is it?

What special name will you give your friend?

Describe the different parts it has.

How will you care for your friend?

CONCEPT MAP

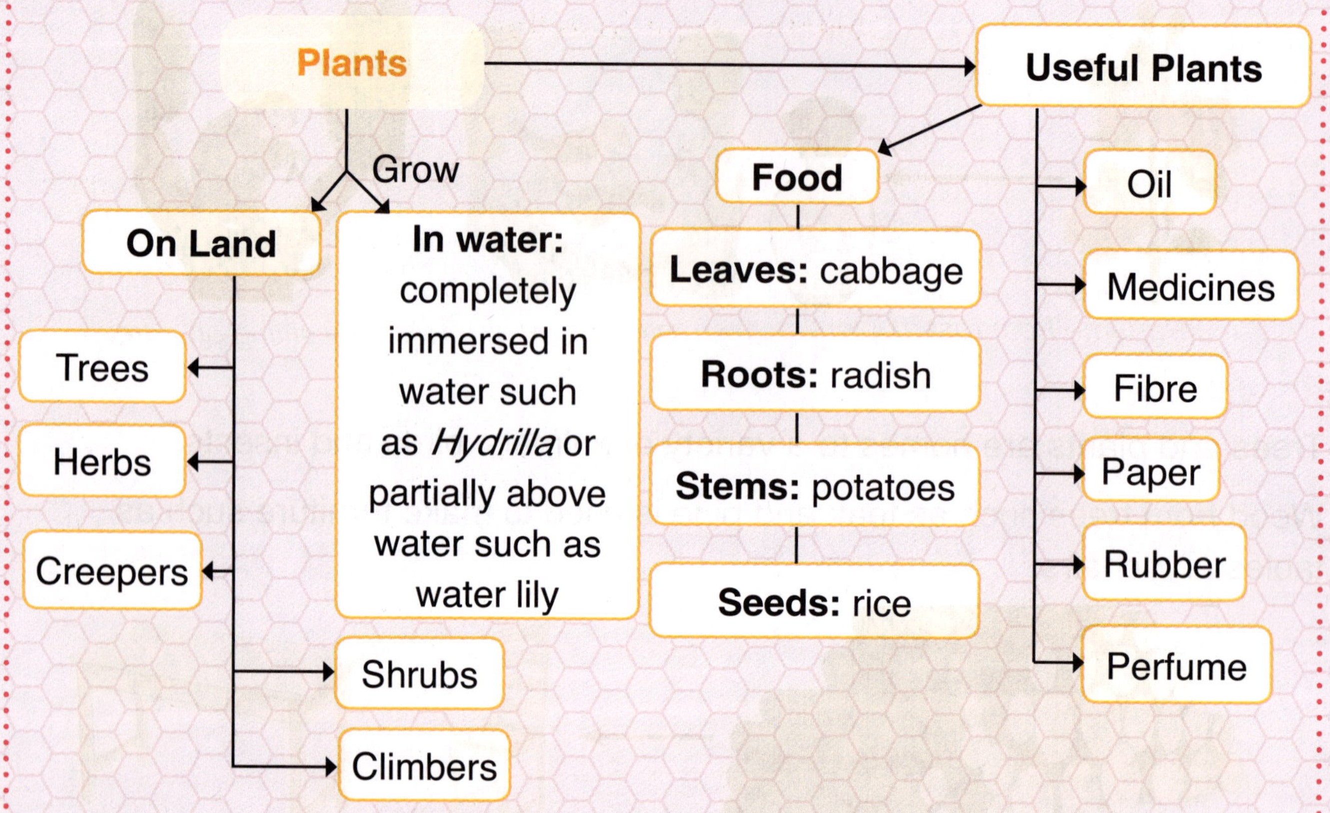

KEYWORDS

Trees: big plants

Shrubs: small plants with many branches

Herbs: small plants with soft, weak and green stems

Climbers: plants with green stems that need support to grow

Creepers: plants with very weak stems that creep on the ground

Exercise

Objective Type Questions

A. Fill in the blanks.

1. __________ (Leaves/Stems) make food for the plant.
2. Plants with soft, weak and green stems are called __________ (trees/herbs).
3. Two seeds that we eat are __________ (*rajma*/apple seed) and __________ (pepper/cabbage).
4. We get __________ (paper/oil) by crushing seeds.

B. Write T for True and F for False.

1. Paper comes from the bamboo plant. ◯
2. Potato is a root. ◯
3. *Hibiscus* plant is a shrub. ◯
4. Flowers carry water and food for the plant. ◯

C. Give two examples of the following.

1. Stems we eat __________ __________
2. Roots we eat __________ __________
3. Leaves we eat __________ __________
4. Seeds we eat __________ __________

Subjective Type Questions

Answer the following questions.

1. Name the different parts of a plant.

____

____

2. Write any four uses of plants.

____

____

Application-based Question

Who is a vegetarian? How is being a vegan different from being a vegetarian?

Picture-based Question

Identify the type of plant given below.

1. ____________ 2. ____________ 3. ____________ 4. ____________ 5. ____________

Skill Booster

A. 21CS: Creativity and Innovation | AI | CC: Physical Education | BT: Cognitive, Psychomotor

Go on a nature walk. Collect leaves, flowers and seeds that have fallen on the ground (do not pluck them from the plants). Stick the collected items on a chart paper and make a nice design (collage).

B. 21CS: Life Skills | CC: English | BT: Cognitive

Go shopping with an elder and make a list of pulses, spices, oils and other things they buy to use at home. It will be fun to find out the local names and the English names of the items.

Local name	English name

C. 21CS: Critical Thinking | BT: Cognitive

You have learned that paper comes from trees. We should save paper so that we can save trees from being cut.

Can you suggest any two ways to save paper?

Worksheet 10

Sohan eats a variety of fruits every day. He even eats the fruits that he does not like. One day at the market, he wanted to have a plate of cut fruits that had all his favourite fruits. However, his father did not allow him to eat such fruits that were cut and kept in the open at the market.

My SEE Journal

A. Why did Sohan's father give him fruits to eat every day?

____

____

____

____

B. Why did Sohan's father not allow him to eat the fruits at the market?

____

____

____

____

My SDG Journal

3 GOOD HEALTH AND WELL-BEING

A. Why did Sohan have fruits which he did not like?

____

____

B. How do fruits which we get in summer help us handle the heat?

____

____

C. Do you regularly eat all the fruits and vegetables served at home?

____

____

11 Animals

Prior Knowledge

- Names of animals around us
- Animals live on land, in water or trees
- Birds have wings and feathers

Learning Objectives

- Animal characteristics
- Body parts of pet animals
- Life cycle of a butterfly
- Care for pets and other animals
- Places where animals live
- Food that animals eat

LET'S GET STARTED

Look at the shadows and guess the names of the animals.

1. C ___ ___

2. R ___ ___ S ___ ___ R

3. H ___ ___ ___ E

4. M ___ ___ ___ ___

CHARACTERISTICS OF ANIMALS

Animals are living things. They breathe, move, eat, feel, produce babies and grow old.

A kitten grows into a cat

A cow eats grass

Hen with chicks

PET ANIMALS

Animals that are kept at home such as dogs, cats, rabbits, birds, etc. are called **pets**.

Cat

Rabbit

Dog

Parrot

We play with our pets. We also love them and look after them.

TALK TIME

If you had to choose a pet, which animal would you choose and why?

Body Parts of Pet Animals

Can you name the body parts of these pets?

Dog

Fish

Bird

LIFE CYCLE OF A BUTTERFLY

A butterfly lays tiny **eggs** on a leaf. When an egg hatches, a **caterpillar** comes out. It looks like a worm with many legs. The caterpillar eats the leaves of the plants around it. Soon, it makes a hard shell called a **cocoon** around itself. After a few days, a colourful **butterfly** comes out of the cocoon.

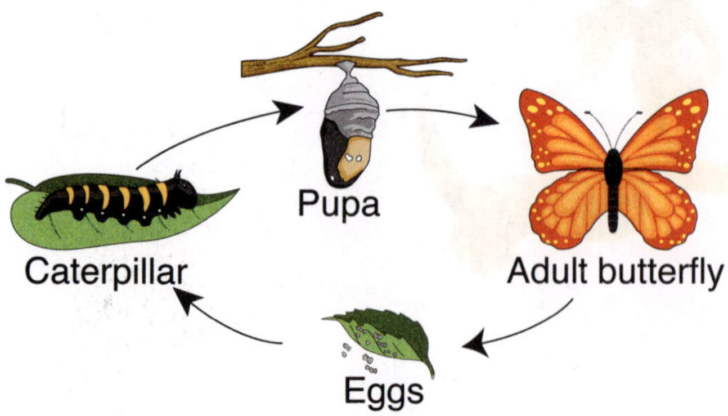

Life cycle of a butterfly

DO YOU KNOW?

Animals such as elephants, mules, donkeys and camels help us by carrying loads for us. So, we must look after them, give them proper food, a comfortable home and allow them to rest.

CARE FOR PETS AND OTHER ANIMALS

We must take care of our pets and farm animals.
So, we must

- bathe them.
- feed them good and healthy food.
- keep their shelter clean.
- take them to a vet when they fall sick.
- be kind to them and love them.

Taking care of pets

QUICK REVISION

What will you do when your pet is

hungry? ____________________

feeling hot or cold? ____________________

hurt or sick? ____________________

teased by someone? ____________________

WILD ANIMALS

Animals that live in a forest and cannot be kept at home are called wild animals. For example, elephant, giraffe, lion and tiger. Wild animals can be big or small in size.

Giraffe

Elephant

Lion

Tiger

WILD ANIMALS AND THEIR HOMES

Some wild animals live on trees. For example, birds, squirrels and monkeys.

Animals that live on trees

Some wild animals live in **burrows**, dens and caves.

WORD TO KNOW

burrow: a wide hole in the ground

Rabbits live in a burrow

Tiger lives in a den

Bear lives in a cave

Some wild animals such as snakes, hares and moles live in holes.

Some wild animals live on both land and in water. For example, crocodile.

Snake lives in a hole

Crocodile lives on land and in water

FIND OUT

Which food do the following animals like to eat?

WHAT DO WILD ANIMALS EAT?

Some animals eat only plants, leaves or grass. They are called **plant-eating animals**.

For example, rhinoceros, deer, horse, elephant and zebra.

Rhinoceros

Zebra

DO YOU KNOW?

Hippopotamus is a plant-eating animal.

Some animals kill other animals and eat their flesh. These are called **flesh-eating animals**. For example, tiger, lion, wolf and cheetah. An eagle is a flesh-eating bird.

Lion

Some wild animals such as bears and crows eat both plants and the flesh of other animals. Some wild animals such as the hyena and vulture eat the flesh of dead animals.

Bear eating a fish

Bear eating a plant

Vulture

Hyena

CONCEPT MAP

Animals

- **Types**
  - **Pet**: Dog, Cat
  - **Wild**: Lion, Tiger
- **What do they eat?**
  - Plant-eating: Deer
  - Flesh-eating: Wolf
  - Both plant and flesh: Bear
  - Flesh of dead animals: Hyena

KEYWORDS

Pets: animals that are kept at home

Life cycle: stages that a living thing goes through during its lifetime

Wild animals: animals that live in a forest

Plant-eating animals: animals that eat only plants

Flesh-eating animals: animals that hunt other animals and eat their flesh

Exercise

Objective Type Questions

A. Group the animals according to their eating habits.

deer, cheetah, zebra, tiger, wolf, horse, elephant, lion, eagle, giraffe

Plant-eating animals	Flesh-eating animals
....	....
....	....
....	....
....	....
....	....

B. Group the animals according to where they live.

bird, lion, moles, bear, squirrel, rabbit, tiger, monkey, snake

In holes/burrows	On trees	In caves/dens
....	....	....
....	....	....
....	....	....

Subjective Type Questions

Answer the following questions.

1. What are wild animals? Give any two examples.

____

2. Name any two animals that eat both plants and flesh of other animals.

____

3. Name two animals that eat the flesh of dead animals.

____

4. How do you look after a pet animal?

____

Application-based Question

What do you think will happen if all the vultures and hyenas disappear from the jungle?

Picture-based Question

Label the different stages of life cycle of a butterfly.

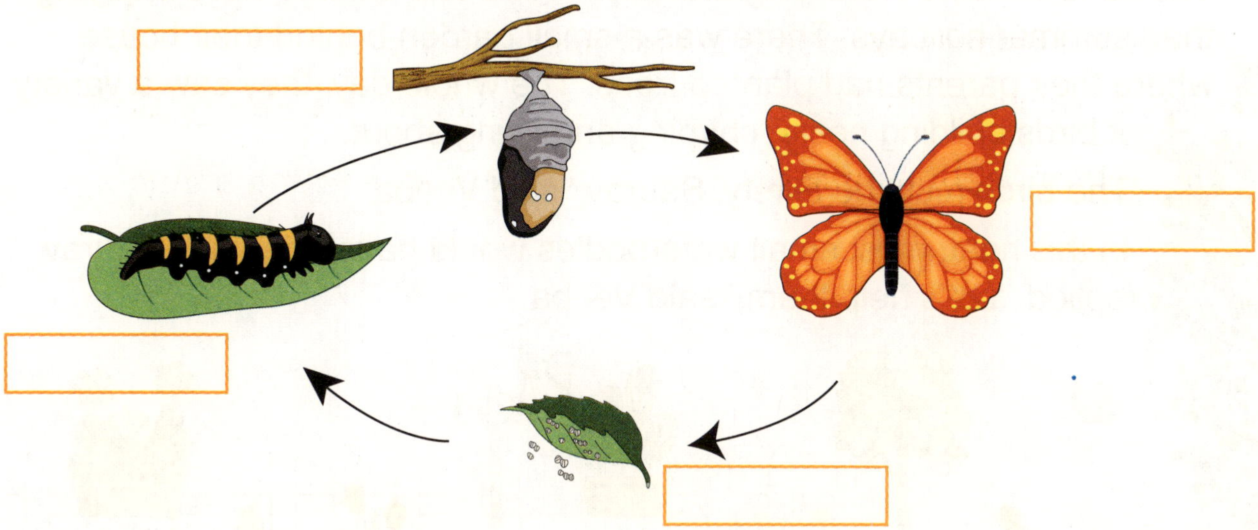

Skill Booster

A. 21CS: Information Literacy | BT: Cognitive

Collect pictures of five flesh-eating and five plant-eating animals and paste them in your scrapbook. Write a line about each animal.

B. 21CS: Critical Thinking | BT: Cognitive, Affective

We know that wild animals live in forests. Sometimes, elephants enter villages and destroy houses. Monkeys also come to towns in large groups and trouble people. Do you know why these things happen? Discuss with your friends to find a solution.

Worksheet 11

The summer days were long and hot. Veeba and Saurav were enjoying their summer holidays. There was a small garden behind their house where their parents had planted trees. The whole day, they saw a variety of birds building nests, chirping and flying about.

'The birds must be thirsty, Saurav,' said Veeba.

'In this heat, most small waterbodies would have dried up,' Saurav replied. 'Let's help them,' said Veeba.

My SEE Journal

A. How do you think the children helped the thirsty birds?

B. Which animals in our neighbourhood suffer from thirst in the summer days?

C. What quality do the two children show?

My SDG Journal

A. What are the things in your neighbourhood which may be a cause of the suffering to animals?

B. How can you make your neighbourhood a better place for the animals living there?

12 Transport

Prior Knowledge

- Types of transport
- Traffic lights

Learning Objectives

- City transport
- Causes of traffic jam
- What makes air dirty?
- Ways to save fuel

LET'S GET STARTED

In Class 1, we learnt about various vehicles we use for transport. Can you think of a form of transport that has the following. Complete the table.

Two wheels	Four wheels	Many wheels	Runs on electricity

MEANS OF TRANSPORT

In the olden days, people travelled from place to place on foot. They carried their goods on the back of animals.

Horse

Camel

Ox

It was the discovery of the wheel, which made life easier for them. The ancient people even made rafts joining the logs and used them to move on water.

Today, we have many different types of transport to take us from one place to another in a shorter amount of time and with great speed.

Vehicles that help us to go from one place to another or help us to carry goods are called **means of transport.**

LAND TRANSPORT

There are two means of land transport—road and rails. Vehicles such as bus, car, bicycle, motorcycle, truck, lorry, jeep and auto rickshaw move on roads. These form a part of the roadways.

Trains, trams, metro trains, etc. move on tracks and form a part of the railways.

Bus

Cycle

Rickshaw

Train

AIR TRANSPORT

Aeroplanes and helicopters are the means of air transport. An aeroplane carries people and goods over a long distance in the shortest possible time. Helicopters can take people to places where there is no airport.

A space shuttle is used to travel into space.

Aeroplane

WATER TRANSPORT

Boat

Yacht

Ships, boats, yachts, rafts, canoes and kayaks are some means of water transport. They move on water. Heavy things are carried across the water to different countries in a ship. Yachts and ships can also carry people from one place to another. However, they take longer time.

QUICK REVISION

Fill in the blanks.

1. A rickshaw is a means of ______________ (water/land) transport.
2. A train moves on the ______________ (road/track).
3. An aeroplane carries people over a long distance in the ______________ (shortest/longest) possible time.
4. ______________ (Yachts/Ships) are used to carry heavy things across the water.

CITY TRANSPORT

In a city, which has many people, we have different kinds of transport. Some common ones are buses, cars, auto rickshaws, scooters, motorbikes and lorries. Underground trains, metros and local trains help people travel across the city very fast. People can also hire a taxi to move from one place to another. An ambulance carries sick people to the hospital.

Causes of Traffic Jam in a City

- In big cities, thousands of cars move on roads at the same time. This leads to a traffic jam.
- Sometimes, the roads are narrow and cars cannot move very easily. This also leads to a traffic jam.

TALK TIME

Which means of transport do you use to travel to your school? Can you think of some other means of transport used in a city?

- In some places, we have fast-moving and slow-moving vehicles moving together, which adds to the traffic jam.

Traffic jam in a city

The traffic policemen help to clear jams. Drivers should obey traffic signals and follow traffic rules to avoid traffic jams.

Vehicles give out smoke that is **poisonous** and makes the air dirty. We should get our cars regularly checked to stop them from giving out smoke, which is bad for our health and causes breathing problems.

WORD TO KNOW
poisonous: harmful

A vehicle giving out smoke

We should not blow the horn unless needed, as loud honking adds to the noise. Have you seen a no horn sign outside a school or a hospital?

No horn signboard

Traffic noise

FUEL FOR CARS

Fuels are the materials that make a car run. Cars run on petrol and diesel. Petrol and diesel are sold at petrol pumps.

Have you seen an auto rickshaw that is bright green in colour?

Well, these bright green auto rickshaws do not run on petrol or diesel. They run on CNG (Compressed Natural Gas), which is good for the environment. They do not give out black smoke and cause less harm to the environment.

Auto

Ways to Save Petrol/Diesel

- When going to a nearby place, walk instead of taking the car.
- While travelling to school, office, or when you are going to a party, it is better to carpool, as that saves fuel.
- While on the road, you must switch off the engine when the car is standing.

GREENATHON

Earth has a fixed amount of petrol and diesel. So, we must use it carefully.

CONCEPT MAP

- Transport
  - Land Transport
    - **On road:** Lorry, Bus, Car
    - **On tracks:** Trains, Metro
  - Air Transport: Aeroplane, Helicopter
  - Water Transport: Ship, Boat

KEYWORDS

Land transport: vehicles that move on the land

Air transport: vehicles that move in air

Water transport: vehicles that move on water

Fuel: materials that make a car run

CNG: compressed natural gas

Exercise

Objective Type Questions

A. Choose the correct answer.

1. __________ needs an airport to land.

   a. Helicopter b. Aeroplane c. Bus d. Boat

2. To reach the moon, we need to travel in a __________.

   a. submarine b. space shuttle c. helicopter d. bus

3. You get petrol from a __________.

   a. garage b. petrol pump c. river d. soil

4. A __________ can carry many people at the same time.

   a. metro b. bicycle c. bike d. rickshaw

B. Put the following under correct the heading.

fighter plane ship helicopter hot air balloon
rickshaw train yacht submarine tram

Land	Air	Water

Subjective Type Questions

Answer the following questions.

1. Name three different kinds of transport. Give examples.

   ____

2. What causes traffic jams? Give two reasons.

   ____

3. How can you save petrol?

   ____

Application-based Question

Why does an ambulance use a loud siren?

Picture-based Question

Join the dots to draw the means of transport and name it.

Skill Booster

A. 21CS: Critical Thinking | BT: Cognitive

How would you go to these places from your home?

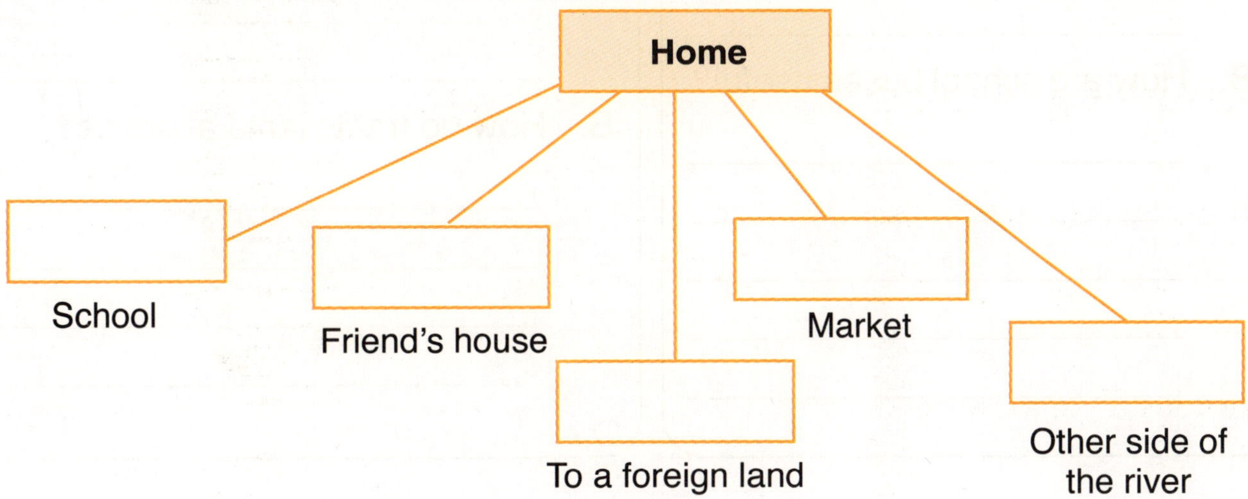

Worksheet 12

Satish takes a lot of time to return home from school. His mother goes to pick him up by car. There are three schools in the same locality, which get over at the same time. Every afternoon, there is a huge line of cars on all the roads near the schools.

My SEE Journal

A. What do you think will happen if four or five students living in the same area use the same car to go home?

B. How are school buses useful?

My SDG Journal

11 SUSTAINABLE CITIES AND COMMUNITIES

A. How do you travel to and from the school? Is there any way in which you can help to lessen the condition on the roads and air pollution?

B. How do traffic jams affect us?

13 Communication

Prior Knowledge

- How to communicate
- Different ways to communicate

Learning Objectives

- Need for communication
- Ways of communication
- Uses of communication
- Communication for recreation
- Ways to check misuse of communication devices

LET'S GET STARTED

Look at the picture given below and answer the questions.

What are the people doing?

____

Are they talking to each other?

____

Do you think that what they are doing is polite?

____

NEED FOR COMMUNICATION

We all need to communicate and speak to each other, as well as share our feelings and ideas. We can get very lonely if we do not have anyone to speak with.

DO YOU KNOW?

The first written communication was in the form of marks and symbols, which was recorded more than 9000 years ago.

WAYS OF COMMUNICATION

In Class 1, we learned about the different means of communication. Let us recall them. Look at the pictures given in each box.

Box A

Computer

Telephone

Mobile phone

Laptop

Box B

Radio

Television

Newspaper

Letter

Magazines

Books

Box A has pictures of different kinds of gadgets and machines. We use these gadgets to communicate and talk to each other.

Box B has another way of sharing news and ideas. These means of communication spread the information to many people at the same time. This type of communication is called **mass communication**.

GREENATHON

If all our newspaper was recycled, we could save about millions of trees each year!

QUICK REVISION

Write T for True and F for False.

1. We do not need to communicate with others. ◯
2. We use telephone for communicating with others. ◯
3. We can directly share news with other person with the help of newspaper. ◯

USE OF COMMUNICATION

DO YOU KNOW?
The first computer mouse ever made was made of wood.

Nowadays, we use machines such as computers, laptops, mobile phones and tablets to communicate with each other. All these machines need the Internet to function. It is the quickest way to communicate with people across the world. We send an e-mail or an SMS and get an instant reply. We can make video calls and speak to our friends and family anywhere in the world and share pictures and videos with them.

We can get any information we want in a minute through the Internet.

COMMUNICATION FOR RECREATION

We see people busy on their mobile phones reading messages, listening to music and watching movies on it. People also play computer games to keep themselves busy.

Boy listening to music

WAYS TO CHECK MISUSE OF COMMUNICATION

Spending too much time over the computer is not healthy.

We must not spend all our free time on the computer, laptop and mobile phone playing games.

When we only stay indoors and play on our computer, we will no longer remain fit and healthy. We need to go out and meet friends and play games that can help us stay fit and healthy.

We must use computers and communication gadgets carefully and not misuse them.

CONCEPT MAP

Communication

- To each other
  - Example: Telephone, mobile phone, computer and laptop
- Sharing ideas or news with many
  - Example: Radio, television, newspaper and magazines

KEYWORDS

Communication: sharing of ideas and feelings

SMS: short message service

Internet: computer network

E-mail: electronic mail

Misuse: wrong use

Exercise

Objective Type Questions

A. Choose the correct answer.

1. Another word for speaking to each other is ____________.

   a. Internet b. communicate c. ICT d. newspaper

2. ____________ can be used to send messages to many people at the same time.

   a. Radio b. Telephone c. Mobile phone d. Laptop

3. We can get information on any topic through the ____________.

   a. magazine b. Internet c. newspaper d. radio

B. Unscramble the letters to find the means of communication.

OETRCMPU ____________

RSTTLEE ____________

EEEPTNHOL ____________

ZAAGMENI ____________

C. Circle the odd one out.

1. Computer, telephone, mobile phone, i-pad
2. Radio, letters, magazine, newspaper

Subjective Type Questions

Answer the following questions.

1. Name the gadgets that we can use to communicate with people who are far away from us.

   ____

   ____

   ____

2. How can we spread news to many people at the same time?

   ____

   ____

   ____

Application-based Question

An earthquake warning has to be given to the people. How can we communicate it to all the people of the city immediately?

Picture-based Question

It's your friend's birthday next week and you want to send him or her a greeting card. Look at the picture of an envelope given below. Write your friend's name and address on it.

Skill Booster

21CS: Information Literacy | **AI** | **BT:** Cognitive

On a chart paper, draw or paste pictures of the different means of communication. Write whether the means of communication is a direct way of sharing news with others or an indirect way.

Worksheet 13

Ruma and Shruti are best friends. They are neighbours and classmates. During summer holidays each year, Shruti goes to Kanpur for two weeks to spend time with her grandparents. This year, Ruma's cousin got married and Shruti's family could not attend because they were in Kanpur.

'I am really, really missing you,' sighed Ruma on the phone.

'I am missing the good food, dressing up and the celebrations!' said Shruti. 'You have to send me pictures and videos of everything!'

My SEE Journal

A. Ruma wanted to share all the news of how she was enjoying the wedding celebrations with Shruti. How did she do that?

B. Why did Ruma miss Shruti at the wedding?

My SDG Journal

9 INDUSTRY, INNOVATION AND INFRASTRUCTURE

A. Many of Ruma's relatives live abroad. How do you think the wedding invitations were sent to them?

B. Was Shruti able to see the wedding photos? How?

14 The World Around Me: Sun, Moon, Sky and Stars

Prior Knowledge

- Things that we see in the sky
- Weather changes every day
- Seasons

Learning Objectives

- Changes seen in the sky during the day, afternoon and night time
- Solar system and other heavenly bodies
- Day and night formation

LET'S GET STARTED

Look at the pictures and answer the question.

1

2

Is the morning sky different from the night sky? How?

____

____

____

THE SKY

On a sunny day, the sky looks blue.

The sun shines brightly.

On a rainy day, the sky looks dark.

The sun hides behind the clouds.

At night, the moon shines in the sky.

We also see many stars twinkling in the sky.

The Earth, the moon and the sun are called heavenly bodies. There are many other heavenly bodies.

We live on the Earth. It is a planet. Planets move around the sun. There are eight planets—Mercury, Venus, Earth, Mars, Jupiter, Saturn, Uranus and Neptune. These planets, the moon, other heavenly bodies and the sun form the **solar system**.

① Mercury
② Venus
③ Earth
④ Mars
⑤ Jupiter
⑥ Saturn
⑦ Uranus
⑧ Neptune

Solar system

QUICK REVISION

Fill in the blanks.

1. On a sunny day, the sky looks ______________ (blue/dark).
2. The sun hides behind the clouds on a ______________ (sunny/rainy) day.
3. At night, the ______________ (moon/sun) shines in the sky.
4. There are ______________ (eight/nine) planets in our solar system.

EARTH

The Earth is our home.

Earth is the only planet known to have life on it.

Earth

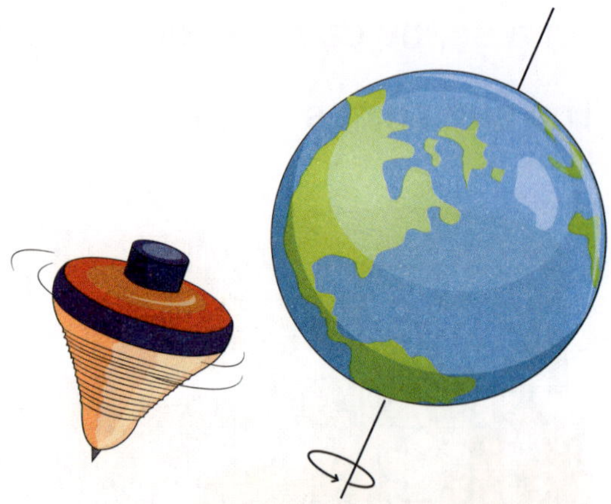

Earth spins like a top

Earth spins like a top from the west to east. This is called **rotation**. It takes 24 hours to complete one rotation. Rotation of the Earth causes day and night. The part of the Earth that faces the sun has day. The other half of the Earth that is away from the sun has night.

Earth revolves around the sun

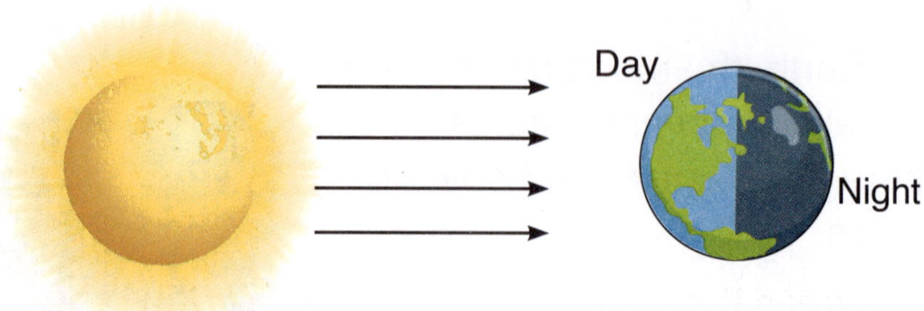

Day and night

The Earth also moves around the sun. This is called a **revolution**. It takes 365 days, 5 hours, 59 minutes and 16 seconds to complete one revolution. The revolution of the Earth around the sun causes the change of seasons.

CONCEPT MAP

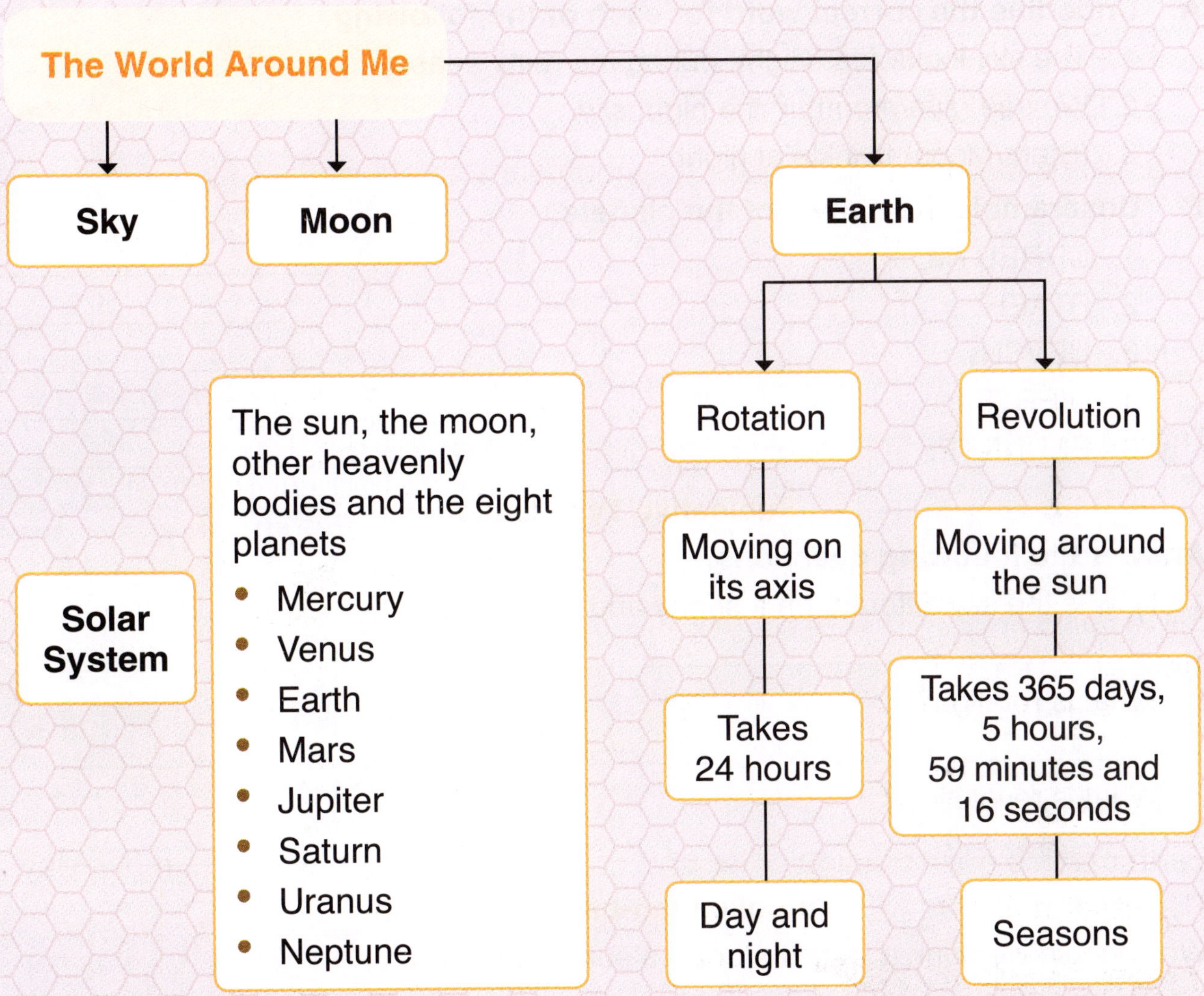

KEYWORDS

Rotation: spinning of the Earth that causes day and night

Revolution: movement of the Earth around the sun

Seasons: spring, summer, monsoon, autumn and winter

Solar System: the sun, the eight planets that move around the sun, the moon and other heavenly bodies

Exercise

Objective Type Questions

A. Underline the correct word for each of the following.

1. The sky looks (dark/light) during the rainy season.
2. We see (sun/moon) in the night sky.
3. (Stars/Moon) twinkle at night.

B. Unscramble the names of the planets.

1. CRREUYM: ____________
2. RTAEH: ____________
3. UEVSN: ____________
4. UIERTPJ: ____________
5. EEUNNTP: ____________

Subjective Type Questions

Answer the following questions.

1. How is the sky different on a sunny and a rainy day?

____

2. What is rotation?

____

3. What is revolution?

____

Application-based Question

Why should we drink a lot of water on a sunny day?

Picture-based Question

Draw to show a glimpse of the sky during the day and at night.

Skill Booster

A. 21CS: Creativity and Innovation | AI | BT: Psychomotor

Take a chart paper. Redraw the Solar System given below. Label the planets in a creative way.

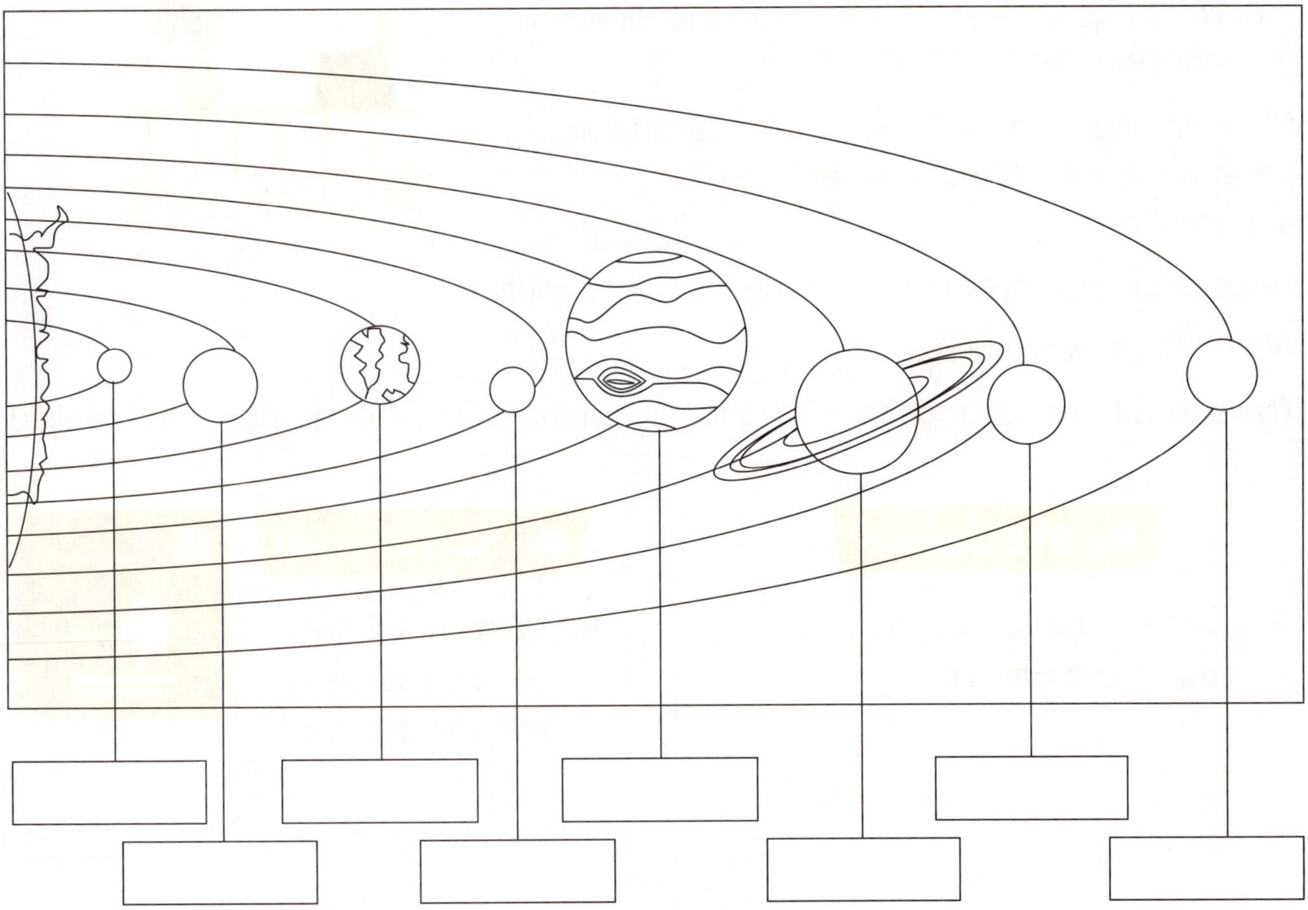

B. 21CS: Information Literacy | CC: English | BT: Cognitive

Find sky words like the one given below.

1. A bird: SKY LARK
2. A high window in the roof made for light and air to come in: SKY ____________
3. A sport: SKY ____________
4. A very tall building: SKY ____________

Worksheet 14

Diya's grandparents had come to stay with them for a few weeks. One morning, Diya woke up very early just as the sun was rising. She heard someone chanting right outside her window. She climbed out of bed and looked outside. She saw her grandmother offering prayers in the direction of the rising sun.

While having breakfast, Diya asked Grandma, 'What were you chanting so early in the morning?'

'I was offering prayers to the rising sun,' she replied.

'Why?' Diya was curious.

'The sun is the most important thing for life on the Earth,' her grandmother replied.

My SEE Journal

A. Why is the sun so important to us on the Earth?

B. What are the heavenly bodies that you see in the night sky?

C. How do you feel when you look up at the night sky and see the stars?

My SDG Journal

15 LIFE ON LAND

A. Which animals and birds sleep during the day and hunt at night?

B. How do sunrise and sunset affect the birds?

15 Time, Space and Direction

Prior Knowledge

- Days of the week
- Months of the year
- The names of four directions

Learning Objectives

- Days, weeks, months and years
- Yesterday, today and tomorrow
- Space
- Direction
- Location of places in the surroundings

LET'S GET STARTED

1. Write three things you do in the morning.

____

____

____

2. Write three things you do at night.

____

____

____

Time is very important to all of us. We try to do all our activities on time. In olden days, people used to keep track of time by looking at the position of the sun. Now, we have clocks and watches that help us know the time.

A POEM!

I hear tick tock, tick tock.
Is it the sound of the clock?
Just to tell me wake up
And go for a walk.

Tick tock, tick tock!
Do I still hear the sound?
I am tired but not the clock
As the hands go round!

A DAY

In the **morning** when the sun rises, a new day begins. Everything looks bright. You go to school in the morning.

> **DO YOU KNOW?**
> The sun rises in the east and sets in the west.

At noon, the sun is just above our head. It is **afternoon**.

The time when the sun is about to set is called **evening**. Once the sun sets, **night** sets in and it becomes dark. We see the moon and the stars in the sky at night.

Morning

Evening

Afternoon

Night

> **DO YOU KNOW?**
> **Dawn** is the first appearance of light before sunrise. **Dusk** is the time when the sun is setting and it is not completely dark.

QUICK REVISION

Write the names of the days of the week

__________ __________ __________ __________

__________ __________ __________

We measure time in **hours, minutes** and **seconds**.

The hands on a clock help us read time. There are two hands—one long and one short. The long hand shows the minutes, while the short hand shows the hours.

DO YOU KNOW?

The letter 'd' is silent when you say Wednesday.

Day, Week, Month and Year

A day has 24 hours.

60 seconds = 1 minute

60 minutes = 1 hour

24 hours = 1 day

7 days = 1 week

12 months = 1 year

365 days = 1 year

366 days = 1 leap year (A year with an extra day, which is 29 February. A leap year comes every four years.) 1 month has 28, 30 or 31 days. A year has 52 weeks.

Yesterday, Today, Tomorrow

What day is it **today**? ____________________

The day before today is **yesterday**.

So, what day was yesterday? ____________________

The day after today is **tomorrow**.

So, what day will **tomorrow** be? ____________________

QUICK REVISION

Fill in the blanks.

1. When the sun is right above our head, it is __________.
2. A __________ begins when the sun rises.
3. Day turns into __________ when the sun sets.

SPACE

To locate or find the position of a place or thing, we use many words such as left, right, near, far, below, above, in and on.

Follow the instructions to complete the picture. Then colour it.

- Draw a cat sitting on the chair.
- Draw a boy to the right of the table.
- Draw a dog under the chair.
- Draw a picture frame above the table.
- Draw a water bottle inside the bag.
- Draw a ruler to the left of the book.

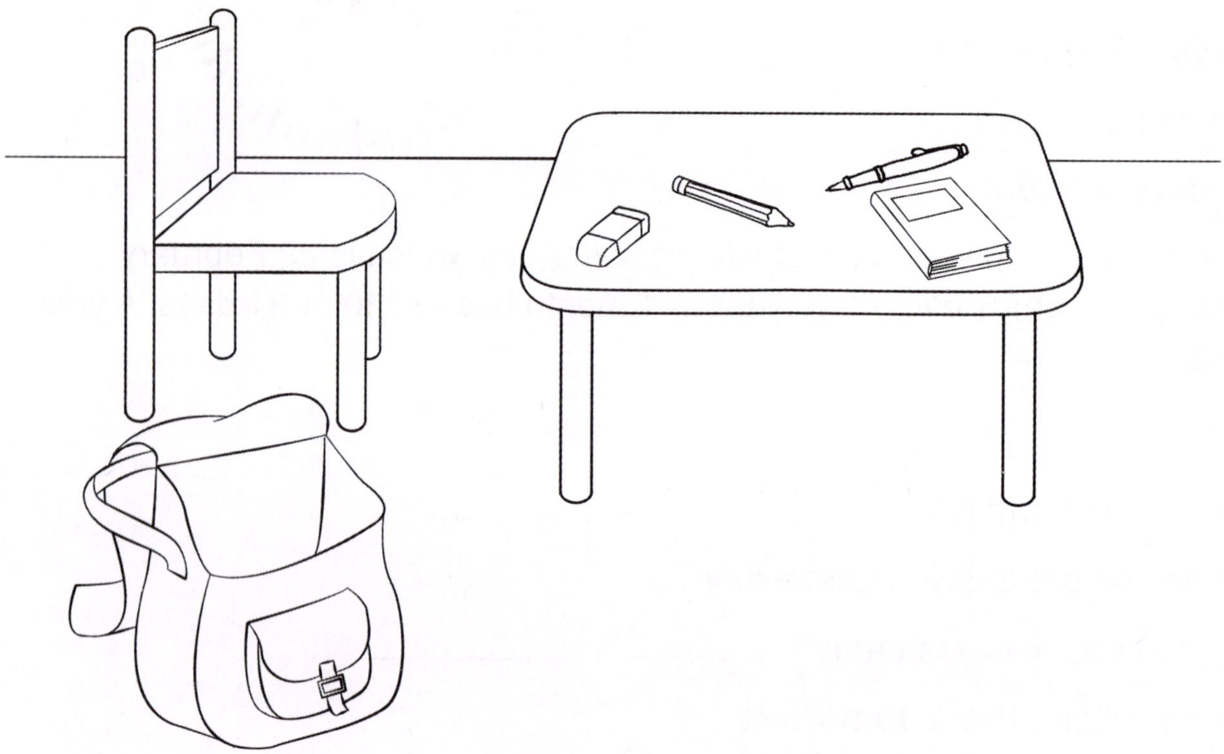

DIRECTIONS

There are four main directions: **North**, **South**, **East** and **West**.

We know that the sun rises in the East.

The sun sets in the West.

If we go out in the morning and stand facing the sun, we would be facing the East. Behind us would be the West.

Now, if we stretch out our arms, to our right would be the South and to our left the North.

FIND OUT

- Go out in the open early in the morning to see the direction in which the sun is rising.
- Once again, in the evening, find out the direction in which the sun is setting.

DO YOU KNOW?

A compass is an instrument used to find out directions.

Fill the directions in the picture below.

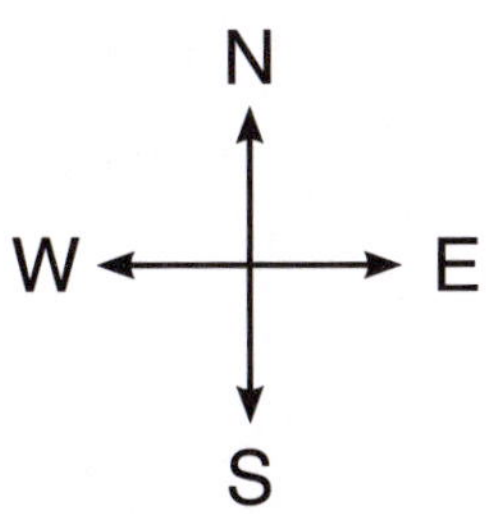

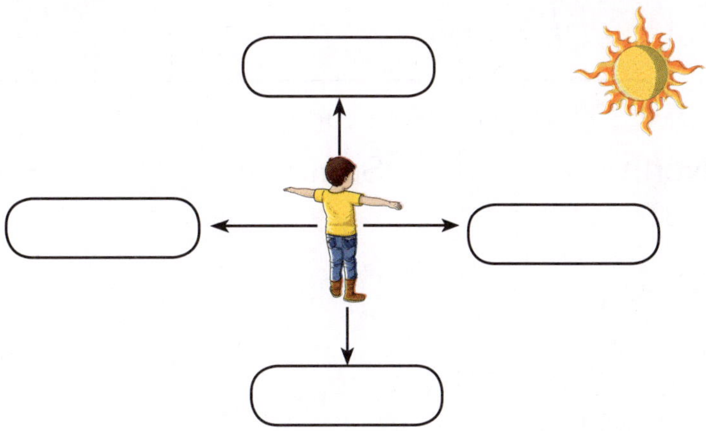

WHERE AM I?

Look at me standing in the centre!

- The school is to the ____________ of me.
- To my ____________ is the pond.
- The park is to the ____________ of me.
- The tree is to the ____________ of me.

CONCEPT MAP

Time

- Morning
- Afternoon
- Evening
- Night

- Day
- Week
- Month
- Year

Directions

- North
- South
- East
- West

KEYWORDS

Evening: the time when the sun is about to set at the end of the day
Night: darkness after sunset
Yesterday: the day before
Tomorrow: the day after
Directions: north, south, east and west

Exercise

Objective Type Questions

A. Fill in the blanks.

1. A day has ____________ (24/12) hours.
2. The last day of the week is ____________ (Saturday/Sunday).
3. 60 seconds make a/an ____________ (minute/hour).
4. The sun sets in the ____________ (east/west).
5. The ____________ (long/short) hand on a clock face tells us the hour.

B. Name the following.

1. Tells us time ____________
2. A duration of twelve months ____________
3. An instrument that helps us find directions ____________
4. The day after today ____________

Subjective Type Questions

Answer the following questions.

1. Name the four directions.

____

____

____

2. How is a leap year different from the other years?

____

____

____

3. How can we find the directions by facing the rising sun?

____

____

____

Application-based Question

What helps you in finding the location of your friend's house without knowing the direction?

Picture-based Question

Look at the pictures given below and fill in the blanks.

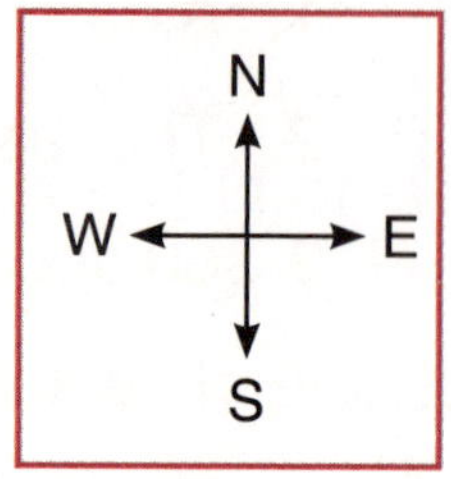

1. The school is to the ______________ of the library.
2. The zoo is to the ______________ of the school.
3. The grocery store is to the ______________ of the hospital.
4. The zoo is to the ______________ of the fire station.

Skill Booster

A. **21CS:** Critical Thinking, Life Skills | **BT:** Cognitive, Psychomotor

Take a compass. Use it to find the directions to the school park.

B. **21CS:** Creativity and Innovation, Collaboration | **CC:** English | **BT:** Cognitive

Form six groups. Each group will make a calendar that shows two months of the year, as mentioned by your teacher. Now, put them up on the soft board and you have an entire calendar for your classroom. After your calendar is complete, use it to unscramble the names of the months given below.

Unscramble the names of the months:
(you may use a calendar, if you are not too sure.)

rhcam:	__________	oeermnbv:	__________	nujaray:	__________
uaustg:	__________	uylj:	__________	ruafbeyr:	__________
pteeerbsm:	__________	irlpa:	__________	nuje:	__________
brectoo:	__________	rebecdme:	__________	yma:	__________

Worksheet 15

The Mathematics teacher had given Anish's class sums to solve at home. Anish's family had to attend a family function that evening. Anish planned to finish the homework before going to the function. However, while playing with his friends, he forgot and came home late.

My SEE Journal

A. Did Anish get the time to do his homework?

B. What should Anish have done to make sure that his homework was done?

My SDG Journal

4 QUALITY EDUCATION

A. Does Anish understand the importance of time?

B. Do you plan the time when you have homework to do?

C. Do you take the help of anything to remind you when there is something important to be done?

Review Corner

Review Corner 1 (Chapters 1–4) **Maximum Marks: 25**

A. Choose the correct answer. (5)

1. This organ gives shape and support to our body.
   a. Bone b. Eyes c. Heart
2. This is a national festival.
   a. Gurpurab b. Gandhi Jayanti c. Diwali
3. This is a Go food.
   a. Meat b. Cheese c. Orange
4. The main source of water is ______________.
   a. pond b. river c. rain
5. India's Republic Day is celebrated on
   a. 2 October b. 26 January c. 15 August

B. Fill in the blanks. (5)

1. A ______________ diet keeps us healthy and fit.
2. Food gives us ______________.
3. ______________ water seeps into the soil.
4. It is important to ______________ drinking water.
5. A small family is called a ______________ family.

C. Answer the following questions. (8)

1. What is a joint family?
2. Write two ways in which you can take care of your body.
3. How can we look after our pet?
4. What are the different sources of water?

D. Name the following. (4)

1. Your mother's mother ______________
2. Festival of lights ______________
3. A place where two bones meet ______________
4. Food that is tasty but not healthy ______________

E. Draw a Grow food, a Glow food and a Go food. (3)

GROW food	GLOW food	GO food

Review Corner 2 (Chapters 5–8)

Maximum Marks: 25

A. Write T for true and F for false. (4)

1. A temporary house used by campers is called an igloo.
2. Silk is an animal fibre.
3. Measles is an airborne disease.
4. A hut is a *kutcha* house.

B. Match the following. (4)

1. A floating house — a. sleep
2. Wool — b. storm
3. Strong wind — c. houseboat
4. Rest — d. animal fibre

C. Fill in the blanks. (5)

1. A ________________ is a house on wheels.
2. ________________ is an artificial fibre.
3. Moving air is called ________________.
4. Plants make the air clean by producing ________________.
5. People carry ________________ during the rainy season.

D. Answer the following questions. (10)

1. Write two ways you can keep your house clean.
2. Why do some houses have sloping roofs?
3. What are natural fibres? Give examples.
4. What makes air dirty?
5. What do you like to do in your free time?

E. **Draw a house with a flat roof and a house with a sloping roof. Where do you find such houses?** (2)

A house with a flat roof	A house with a sloping roof

Review Corner 3 (Chapters 9–12)

Maximum Marks: 25

A. **Write T for true and F for false.** (4)

1. A person who repairs our gas stove is called a postman.
2. Big plants are called trees.
3. Grass and mint are shrubs.
4. Playing with a matchstick is not safe.

B. **Fill in the blanks.** (2)

1. The help given to a person before the doctor arrives is called ________________.
2. Trees have thick stems called ________________.
3. The eggs of a butterfly hatch into a ________________.
4. The ________________ eats the flesh of dead animals.

C. **Match the following.** (4)

1. Medicines	a. mason
2. Potato	b. oil
3. A stone worker	c. paper
4. Bamboo	d. stem
5. Seeds	e. neem

D. Answer the following questions. (10)

1. What are wild animals?
2. How are plants useful to us?
3. How are climbers different from creepers?
4. What do good neighbours do?
5. What are safety rules?

E. Draw and label the parts of a plant. (5)

Review Corner 4 (Chapters 13–15) Maximum Marks: 25

A. Write T for true and F for false. (4)

1. A newspaper can spread a message to many people at a time.
2. Trains need tracks to move on land.
3. A year has 52 weeks.
4. The revolution of the Earth causes seasons.

B. Fill in the blanks. (5)

1. The sun sets in the ________________.
2. The fastest means of transport is ________________.
3. The ________________ of the Earth causes day and night.
4. An instrument that helps us find directions is called a ________________.
5. We can use ________________ on the computer to get any information we want.

C. Name the following. (4)

1. The only planet with life ________________
2. We use this to send an SMS ________________
3. A vehicle that carries sick people to the hospital ________________
4. A year with 366 days ________________

D. Answer the following questions. (8)

1. What is the Solar System?
2. Name the two movements of the Earth.
3. Why do we need to communicate?
4. What causes a traffic jam?

E. Draw yourself facing the rising sun and write down the directions. (4)

My Environment, My Responsibility!

Say No to Plastic Bags!

We read in the news and see on TV how big cities get flooded when it rains. The rainwater cannot flow into drains because of plastic wastes choking the drains' openings. People living in these cities suffer a lot during these rainy days.

A. Do you live in an area where there is waterlogging whenever it rains?

____

B. Find out whether shopkeepers in your neighbourhood market use plastic bags to sell their goods. Is it good or bad to use plastic bags? Why or why not?

____

C. The government has issued a list of single-use plastic items that are banned. Find out what these items are. Name any three.

____

D. Make a colourful poster on 'Do not use plastic bags'.

My Eco Craft: A Newspaper Bag

Things You Need An old newspaper, a rectangular piece of cardboard or hard paper, glue, woollen thread or jute rope

Let's Start:

1. Take a sheet of newspaper. Fold it lengthwise into four parts. Fold the outer two parts so that they meet and overlap in the middle.

2. Glue the two free ends together.

3. Fold one end of the paper as shown here.

4. Open up the folds to form a square as shown here.

5. Now insert a rectangular piece of cardboard or hard paper inside the square so formed.

6. Glue the newspaper over the hard piece of paper carefully.

7. Punch holes at the open end.

8. Tie up the handles.

Decorate your paper bag if you want. Your bag is ready!

Decorate a Cloth Bag

Many items are delivered to our homes in plain cloth bags. With the help of an elder, turn the plain bag into a beautiful bag by decorating it. Write down the things that you need and the steps of your decoration. Draw or paste a picture of your decorated bag.

Things You Need: ____________________

____

____

____

Let's Start: ____________________

____